Practical TensorFlow for LLM Developers:

Crafting Advanced Chatbots, Summarizers, and More -
From Beginner to Master (LLMs Unraveled: Mastering
TensorFlow, Hugging Face, and Beyond)

Matthew D.Passmore

Table of content

I. Introduction to LLMs and TensorFlow

This section lays the groundwork for your journey into the exciting world of Large Language Models (LLMs) and their development using TensorFlow. We'll delve into the core concepts of both, understand why TensorFlow is a powerful tool for LLM development, and equip you with the foundational knowledge to begin building your own LLM applications.

1.1. What are Large Language Models (LLMs)?

LLMs are a type of artificial intelligence (AI) that process and generate human-like text. Imagine a powerful language learner who has devoured massive amounts of text data, from books and articles to code and social media conversations. This data allows LLMs to grasp the nuances of language, including grammar, syntax, and context.

Here are some key capabilities of LLMs:

Text Generation: LLMs can create human-quality text, like poems, code, scripts, musical pieces, emails, and more.
Machine Translation: LLMs can translate languages with high accuracy, understanding the meaning behind the words.
Question Answering: LLMs can answer your questions in a comprehensive and informative way, drawing from their vast knowledge base.

Text Summarization: LLMs can condense lengthy pieces of text into concise summaries, capturing the essential points.

1.2. Why Use TensorFlow for LLM Development?
TensorFlow is a powerful open-source library developed by Google for numerical computation and large-scale machine learning. Here's why it's a great choice for LLM development:

Flexible Architecture: TensorFlow's flexible architecture allows you to build and train complex neural networks, the core building blocks of LLMs.
Scalability: TensorFlow can handle the massive datasets and computational resources required for training LLMs.
Large Community and Resources: TensorFlow benefits from a vast community of developers and a wealth of resources, including tutorials, code libraries, and technical support.
Integration with Hugging Face: TensorFlow integrates seamlessly with Hugging Face, a popular library offering pre-trained LLM models and tools, accelerating your development process.

1.3. Getting Started with TensorFlow and LLM Concepts
This section will provide a hands-on introduction to TensorFlow and fundamental LLM concepts. You'll learn how to:

Set up a TensorFlow development environment.

Write basic TensorFlow code to understand its core functionalities.
Explore essential LLM concepts like text preprocessing, tokenization, and word embeddings.
By the end of this section, you'll have a solid foundation for building your LLM applications with TensorFlow.

1.1. What are Large Language Models (LLMs)?

Large Language Models (LLMs) are a type of artificial intelligence (AI) that excel at processing and generating human-like text. Imagine an incredibly powerful language learner that has been trained on a massive amount of text data, from books and articles to code and social media conversations. This vast exposure allows LLMs to grasp the nuances of language, including grammar, syntax, and context.

Here are some key capabilities of LLMs:

* **Text Generation:** LLMs can create human-quality text formats, like poems, code, scripts, musical pieces, emails, and more. They can be quite creative!

* **Machine Translation:** LLMs can translate languages with high accuracy, going beyond simply swapping words and understanding the meaning behind them.

* **Question Answering:** LLMs can act like super-powered research assistants, answering your questions in a comprehensive and informative way by drawing from their vast knowledge base.

* **Text Summarization:** Information overload? LLMs can condense lengthy pieces of text into concise summaries, capturing the essential points for you.

1.2. Why Use TensorFlow for LLM Development?

why TensorFlow is a powerful tool for developing Large Language Models (LLMs):

Flexible Architecture: TensorFlow's core strength lies in its ability to construct and train complex neural networks. Since neural networks are the fundamental building blocks of LLMs, TensorFlow provides the perfect platform for creating these intricate models.

Scalability: LLMs require massive datasets and significant computational resources for training. TensorFlow is built to handle these demands. It can efficiently utilize powerful hardware like GPUs (Graphics Processing Units) and TPUs (Tensor Processing Units) to accelerate the training process, which can take days or even weeks depending on the model complexity and dataset size.

Large Community and Resources: TensorFlow boasts a vast and active developer community. This means you have access to a wealth of resources, including tutorials, code libraries, and forums for troubleshooting and learning from others. If you encounter challenges, there's a high chance someone else has faced them before and there's a solution waiting to be found.

Integration with Hugging Face: Hugging Face is a popular library offering pre-trained LLM models and tools. TensorFlow integrates seamlessly with Hugging Face, allowing you to leverage these pre-trained models as a starting point for your own LLM development. This can significantly reduce development time and effort, especially for projects that don't require building an LLM from scratch.

In simpler terms, TensorFlow provides the building blocks, the tools, and the supportive community to construct powerful LLMs efficiently. It also allows you to leverage the work of others through Hugging Face, giving you a head start in your development journey.

1.3. Getting Started with TensorFlow and LLM Concepts

This section will equip you with the essentials to kickstart your LLM development journey using

TensorFlow. We'll guide you through setting up your environment, introduce basic TensorFlow functionalities, and explore fundamental LLM concepts that will be the building blocks for your future projects.

Setting Up Your Development Environment
The first step is to create a development environment where you can code and experiment with TensorFlow. Here's a basic outline:

Install Python: TensorFlow requires Python as its foundation. Download and install the latest version of Python from https://www.python.org/downloads/.

Install TensorFlow: Once you have Python, follow the official TensorFlow installation guide (https://www.tensorflow.org/install/pip) to set up TensorFlow for your specific operating system.

Choose a Code Editor or IDE: Select a code editor or Integrated Development Environment (IDE) that suits your preferences. Popular choices include Visual Studio Code, PyCharm, or Jupyter Notebook. These tools will provide a comfortable space to write your TensorFlow code.

Hands-on with TensorFlow Basics
Now that your environment is ready, let's explore some fundamental TensorFlow concepts through code:

Tensors: The core data structure in TensorFlow is the tensor, a multidimensional array of elements. You'll learn how to create, manipulate, and perform operations on tensors.

Variables: Variables hold the trainable parameters of your models. We'll explore how to define and update variables during the training process.

Building Simple Neural Networks: We'll build a basic neural network using TensorFlow's high-level APIs (like Keras) to understand the core structure and functionalities of these networks.

Running Computations: Explore how to run your TensorFlow computations on different hardware like CPUs or GPUs for faster processing.

Understanding LLM Fundamentals
While we've gotten you started with TensorFlow, let's delve into some key LLM concepts that will be crucial for your future projects:

Text Preprocessing: LLMs can't directly understand raw text data. We'll learn techniques like tokenization (breaking text into smaller units) and cleaning to prepare the data for LLM models.

Word Embeddings: Words hold meaning, but computers need a numerical representation. We'll explore how to convert words into numerical vectors (embeddings) that capture their semantic relationships.

Understanding Transformers: The Transformer architecture is the backbone of modern LLMs. We'll introduce the core principles of Transformers and how they excel at processing sequential data like text.

By the end of this section, you'll have a solid foundation in both TensorFlow and LLM concepts. This knowledge will empower you to build more complex LLM applications in the following sections.

II. Building Blocks of LLM Applications

LLMs rely heavily on a type of artificial intelligence called neural networks. These networks are inspired by the structure of the human brain and consist of interconnected layers of artificial neurons. Each neuron processes information and transmits it to other neurons, mimicking how information flows through the brain.

Deep learning is a subfield of machine learning that utilizes these complex neural networks with many layers. Deep learning architectures like convolutional neural networks (CNNs) and recurrent neural networks (RNNs) have proven highly effective in various tasks, including image recognition and natural language processing (NLP). For LLM applications, a specific type of RNN called a Transformer is particularly important, and we'll explore that in more detail later.

Here's a breakdown of why neural networks are crucial for LLMs:

Learning from Data: Neural networks can learn complex patterns from vast amounts of data. This allows LLMs to learn the intricacies of language by processing massive amounts of text data.
Feature Extraction: Neural networks can automatically extract important features from the data. In the context of LLMs, these features could be the relationships between words, sentence structures, and the overall context of a piece of text.

Non-linear Modeling: Real-world data often has non-linear relationships. Neural networks can effectively model these non-linear relationships, allowing LLMs to capture the nuances of human language that may not be easily expressed in linear models.

2. Working with Text Data: Preprocessing and Embedding

Raw text data isn't readily usable by LLM models. Here's how we prepare text data for these models:

Preprocessing: This crucial step involves cleaning the text data by removing irrelevant characters, fixing typos, and converting text to lowercase or uppercase for consistency. Additionally, techniques like stemming (reducing words to their root form) and lemmatization (converting words to their base form) can be applied depending on the specific task.

Tokenization: We need to break down the text into smaller units that the LLM model can understand. This process, called tokenization, typically involves splitting the text into individual words or sentences (tokens) depending on the application.

Word Embeddings: Once we have tokens, we need to convert them into a numerical representation that the LLM model can process. Word embeddings are a powerful technique that maps each word in the vocabulary to a high-dimensional vector. These vectors capture the semantic relationships between words. Words with similar meanings will have similar vector representations in the embedding space.

There are various techniques for generating word embeddings, and pre-trained word embedding models like Word2Vec and GloVe are often used as a starting point. These pre-trained models learn word embeddings from massive datasets and can be fine-tuned for specific LLM applications.

By effectively preprocessing and embedding text data, we bridge the gap between human language and the numerical world that neural networks operate in. This allows LLMs to understand the meaning and context of the text they are processing.

3. Introduction to Transformers: The Architecture Behind Modern LLMs

As mentioned earlier, Transformers are a specific type of neural network architecture that has revolutionized the field of NLP and is the foundation of most modern LLMs. Here's why Transformers are so effective for LLMs:

Attention Mechanism: Unlike traditional RNNs, Transformers utilize an attention mechanism that allows the model to focus on specific parts of the input sequence when processing it. This enables the model to understand the long-range dependencies between words in a sentence, a critical aspect for tasks like machine translation and text summarization.

Parallel Processing: Transformers can process different parts of the input sequence simultaneously, making them much faster than traditional RNNs, which process information sequentially. This parallel processing capability is crucial for handling the massive amounts of data required for training LLMs.

Encoder-Decoder Architecture: Many Transformer-based LLM models utilize an encoder-decoder architecture. The encoder "reads" the input text and creates a contextual representation. The decoder then uses this context to generate the output, like translating a sentence or summarizing a document.

Understanding these building blocks – neural networks, text data preparation, and the Transformer architecture – equips you with the foundational knowledge to construct and train powerful LLM applications. The following sections will delve into specific LLM applications like chatbots and summarizers, where we'll see how these building blocks come together to create real-world functionalities.

2.1. Understanding Neural Networks and Deep Learning

Neural networks and deep learning are the cornerstones of Large Language Models (LLMs). This section breaks down these concepts to equip you with a solid understanding of the magic that happens behind the scenes of these powerful language models.

1. Unveiling Neural Networks: Inspired by the Brain

Imagine a network of interconnected nodes, loosely resembling the structure of the human brain. This is the core idea behind artificial neural networks. These networks consist of artificial neurons, which process information and transmit it to other neurons. Just like neurons in the brain fire and communicate with each other, these artificial neurons work together to learn and solve problems.

Neural networks are built using layers. Information flows from the input layer, through hidden layers, and finally to the output layer. Each layer performs specific calculations on the data it receives, transforming it step-by-step. The more layers a network has, the more complex relationships it can learn from the data.

Here's what makes neural networks so powerful:

Learning from Data: Unlike traditional programming, neural networks don't require explicit instructions. They can learn from vast amounts of data by adjusting the connections between neurons. This allows LLMs to learn the intricacies of language by processing massive amounts of text data.

Adaptability: Neural networks can continuously improve their performance as they are exposed to more data. This is crucial for LLMs, which need to constantly adapt to new information and language styles.

Non-linear Modeling: The real world is full of complexities and non-linear relationships. Neural networks excel at modeling these non-linearities, allowing LLMs to capture the nuances of human language that may not be easily expressed in simpler models.

2. Deep Learning: Building on the Foundation
Deep learning is a subfield of machine learning that utilizes complex neural networks with many layers. These deep architectures have proven highly effective in various tasks, including image recognition, speech recognition, and, of course, natural language processing (NLP) – the domain of LLMs.

Here's why deep learning is particularly valuable for LLMs:

Feature Extraction: Deep neural networks can automatically extract important features from the data. In the context of LLMs, these features could be the relationships between words, sentence structures, and the overall context of a piece of text. The more layers a network has, the more intricate features it can learn.

Increased Accuracy: With more layers, deep learning models can achieve higher levels of accuracy compared to shallower neural networks. This is crucial for LLMs, where tasks like generating human-quality text or translating languages require a deep understanding of language nuances.

Advanced Applications: Deep learning architectures like Transformers (which we'll discuss later) are specifically designed to handle sequential data like text. These advancements allow LLMs to tackle complex NLP tasks with impressive results.

While the inner workings of neural networks can involve complex mathematics, understanding the core concepts equips you to grasp the power they bring to LLM development. The next section will delve into how we prepare text data for these neural networks, making human language understandable by machines.

2.2. Working with Text Data: Preprocessing and Embedding

Large Language Models (LLMs) are whiz kids at language, but they can't directly understand raw text data. This section dives into how we prepare text data for LLMs through preprocessing and embedding techniques, essentially transforming human language into a format these models can comprehend.

1. Preprocessing: Cleaning Up the Textual Mess
Imagine feeding a messy pile of unwashed clothes to a washing machine – the results wouldn't be ideal. Similarly, raw text data often contains inconsistencies and irrelevant information that can hinder LLM performance. Preprocessing is the essential first step where we clean and tidy up the text data. Here are some common preprocessing techniques:

Normalization: This ensures consistency in the text by converting all characters to lowercase or uppercase for uniformity. Additionally, we might remove punctuation marks or special characters that don't hold meaning for the LLM task.

Cleaning: Text data can contain typos, grammatical errors, or irrelevant symbols. Preprocessing techniques like removing extra spaces, fixing typos, and handling abbreviations can improve the quality of the data.

Stop Word Removal: Many words, like "the," "a," or "an," have little meaning on their own. Stop word removal eliminates these common words from the text, allowing the LLM to focus on the more content-rich words. However, stop word removal should be done cautiously, as some stop words can be important depending on the specific task.

Text Lowercasing/Uppercasing: Depending on the LLM application, converting all text to lowercase or uppercase can be beneficial. This ensures consistency and simplifies the model's learning process.

Stemming and Lemmatization: Words often have different variations (e.g., "walk," "walking," "walked"). Stemming reduces words to their root form (e.g., "walk" for all variations). Lemmatization takes it a step further, converting words to their dictionary base form (e.g., "walk" for all variations). The choice between stemming and lemmatization depends on the specific LLM task.

2. Embedding: Bridging the Gap Between Words and Numbers

After preprocessing, we're left with a collection of clean words. But LLMs operate in the world of numbers, not human language. Here's where word embedding comes in – a powerful technique that bridges this gap.

Imagine a map where each word is a location and similar words are positioned close together. Word embedding assigns a unique high-dimensional vector to each word in the vocabulary. These vectors capture the semantic relationships between words. Words with similar meanings will have similar vector representations in this embedding space.

There are various techniques for generating word embeddings, and pre-trained models like Word2Vec and GloVe are popular choices. These models learn word embeddings from massive datasets and can be fine-tuned for specific LLM applications. Here's how word embeddings benefit LLMs:

Semantic Understanding: By capturing semantic relationships, word embeddings allow LLMs to understand the meaning and context of the text they are processing. For instance, the word vectors for "king" and "queen" would be close in the embedding space, reflecting their similar meaning.

Efficient Processing: Numerical vectors are more efficient for computations than words themselves. Word embeddings enable LLMs to process large amounts of text data faster.

Improved Accuracy: By understanding word relationships, LLMs can perform tasks like text generation, machine translation, and summarization with greater accuracy.

By effectively preprocessing and embedding text data, we unlock the power of LLMs to understand and manipulate human language. The following sections will explore how these techniques are applied in real-world LLM applications like chatbots and summarizers.

2.3. Introduction to Transformers: The Architecture Behind Modern LLMs

Large Language Models (LLMs) wouldn't be possible without the groundbreaking Transformer architecture. This section dives into the world of Transformers, explaining why they are the backbone of modern LLMs and how they revolutionized natural language processing (NLP).

Traditional Challenges in NLP
Before Transformers, recurrent neural networks (RNNs) were the dominant architecture for NLP tasks. However, RNNs faced limitations:

Sequential Processing: RNNs process information sequentially, word by word. This can be slow for long sequences and make it difficult to capture long-range dependencies between words in a sentence (e.g., the relationship between a pronoun and its antecedent).
Vanishing Gradient Problem: In RNNs, gradients - the signals used to train the model - can become very small or large as they propagate through the network. This can hinder the learning process, especially in deep RNNs.
These limitations restricted the capabilities of earlier NLP models. Transformers emerged to address these challenges and unlock a new level of performance in NLP tasks.

Unveiling the Transformer Architecture
Transformers introduced a new approach to processing sequential data like text. Here are the key features that make them so effective:

Attention Mechanism: Unlike RNNs, Transformers leverage an attention mechanism. This allows the model to focus on specific parts of the input sequence simultaneously, not just sequentially. Imagine being able to read an entire sentence at once and understand how each word relates to the others. That's the power of attention!

Encoder-Decoder Architecture: Many Transformer-based LLM models utilize an encoder-decoder structure. The encoder reads the input text and creates a contextual representation of the entire sentence. The decoder then uses this context to generate the output, like translating a sentence or summarizing a document.

Parallel Processing: Transformers can process different parts of the input sequence concurrently. This makes them significantly faster than RNNs, especially for handling massive amounts of text data used to train LLMs.

Self-Attention: A specific type of attention mechanism called self-attention allows the Transformer to understand the relationships between all words in the input sequence, not just neighboring words. This is crucial for tasks like question answering or summarization, where understanding the context of the entire sentence is essential.

The Transformer Revolution

The introduction of Transformers led to a significant leap forward in NLP capabilities. LLMs built on Transformer architectures achieve state-of-the-art performance in various tasks, including:

Machine Translation: Transformers can translate languages with exceptional accuracy, capturing the nuances and context of the source language.
Text Summarization: LLMs can condense lengthy pieces of text into concise summaries that accurately convey the main points.

Question Answering: Transformers can answer your questions in a comprehensive and informative way, drawing from their vast knowledge base and understanding the intent behind your questions.
Text Generation: LLMs can generate different creative text formats, like poems, code, scripts, and even realistic dialogue for chatbots.

By overcoming the limitations of RNNs, Transformers paved the way for the development of powerful and versatile LLMs that are transforming the way we interact with computers and information. The following sections will delve into how Transformers are utilized in specific LLM applications, showcasing the practical applications of this revolutionary architecture.

III. Crafting Advanced Chatbots

Chatbots have become an increasingly common way to interact with businesses and services online. However, traditional chatbots often lack the sophistication to handle complex conversations or natural language nuances. This section explores how Large Language Models (LLMs) empowered by Transformers can elevate chatbots to a new level of interactivity and understanding.

1. Designing Engaging Chatbot Dialog Flow
Before diving into the technical aspects, let's consider the core of any good conversation: the flow of dialogue. Here are some key elements for designing an engaging chatbot experience:

Identify User Goals: Understand what users want to achieve through their interaction with the chatbot. Common goals might be getting customer support, booking appointments, or simply obtaining information. Craft a Natural Conversation Flow: Design the conversation flow to feel natural and engaging. This includes defining conversation starting points, branching dialogues based on user input, and incorporating appropriate greetings and closings.

Anticipate User Queries: Identify the most common questions or requests users might have and design the chatbot to handle them effectively.
Incorporate Personality (Optional): Depending on the application, consider adding personality to your chatbot

to make it more engaging. Humor, empathy, or a specific brand voice can enhance the user experience.

2. Training Chatbots with TensorFlow and LLM Techniques

Now that you have a well-defined conversation flow, let's see how LLMs and TensorFlow come into play:

Intent Recognition: A crucial aspect of chatbot functionality is understanding the user's intent behind their message. LLMs excel at this task. By training an LLM model on a massive dataset of text conversations and user intents, the chatbot can accurately identify the user's goal in each message. TensorFlow provides the framework to train these intent recognition models.

Entity Extraction: Beyond intent, chatbots often need to extract specific entities from user messages. For instance, in a travel booking scenario, the chatbot might need to identify the destination city and travel dates mentioned by the user. LLMs can be trained to recognize and extract these entities from user queries.

Dialogue Generation: Once the intent and entities are identified, the chatbot needs to respond appropriately. Here's where the power of LLM text generation comes in. TensorFlow allows you to train an LLM model on a vast amount of conversation data, enabling the chatbot to generate natural language responses tailored to the user's intent and the context of the conversation.

Here are some additional considerations for training your chatbot:

Fine-Tuning Pre-trained LLMs: Leverage pre-trained LLM models like GPT-3 or Jurassic-1 Jumbo and fine-tune them on your specific chatbot conversation data. This can significantly reduce training time and effort.

Dialogue Management: Implement a dialogue management system to track the conversation history and context. This allows the chatbot to maintain a coherent conversation flow and avoid repetitive responses.

3. Integrating Chatbots with Real-World Applications
Chatbots powered by LLMs can be integrated into various real-world applications:

Customer Service: LLM-powered chatbots can handle customer inquiries, answer frequently asked questions, and even resolve simple customer issues 24/7, improving customer satisfaction and reducing support costs.

Marketing and Sales: Chatbots can engage website visitors, answer product-related questions, and guide users through the sales funnel, increasing lead generation and conversion rates.
Education and Training: Chatbots can provide personalized learning experiences, answer student

questions, and offer feedback on assignments, making education more interactive and accessible.

Healthcare: Chatbots can help patients schedule appointments, answer basic medical questions, or provide mental health support.

By combining the power of LLMs with well-designed conversation flows, you can create advanced chatbots that provide a natural and efficient way for users to interact with your applications or services. The following sections will explore other applications of LLMs, showcasing the versatility of this technology.

3.1. Designing Chatbot Dialog Flow and Intent Recognition

Large Language Models (LLMs) are revolutionizing the way chatbots interact with users. By enabling chatbots to understand natural language and respond in a comprehensive way, LLMs are creating a more engaging and informative user experience. This section dives into the two crucial aspects of building an effective LLM chatbot: designing a natural conversation flow (dialog flow) and recognizing user intent.

1. Building a User-Centric Conversation Flow

The foundation of any good conversation lies in its flow. Here's how to design a captivating dialog flow for your LLM chatbot:

Identify User Goals: What do users aim to achieve through their chatbot interaction? Typical goals might include:

Customer Support: Getting answers to product or service questions, resolving issues, or requesting assistance.

E-commerce: Making purchases, checking order status, or receiving product recommendations.
Information Retrieval: Finding specific details like business hours, contact information, or booking appointments.

Map the Conversation Journey: Plan the different paths a conversation might take based on user choices and goals. This includes defining:

Entry Points: How users will initiate a conversation with the chatbot (e.g., greetings, welcome messages).
Navigation Options: The ways users can navigate through the conversation (e.g., menus, buttons, keywords).

Branching Logic: How the conversation flow adapts based on user input (e.g., asking clarifying questions, providing different response options).

End Points: How the conversation concludes (e.g., offering help with additional tasks, providing closing remarks).
Craft Natural Language Interactions: Strive for a conversational tone that feels natural and engaging. This includes:

Using clear and concise language.
Incorporating greetings, confirmations, and apologies.
Avoiding overly technical jargon.

Embrace Personality (Optional): Depending on the application, consider adding a touch of personality to your chatbot. Humor, empathy, or a specific brand voice can enhance the user experience. However, ensure the personality aligns with your brand image and target audience.

By planning a user-centric conversation flow, you lay the groundwork for a smooth and engaging chatbot interaction.

2. Understanding User Intent with LLM Power
Now that you have a well-defined conversation flow, let's see how LLMs play a crucial role in understanding what users truly want – their intent behind the message.

Intent Recognition: The Core of Understanding: Intent recognition is the ability of the chatbot to identify the user's goal or purpose in their message. For instance, the user's message "My internet is down. Can you help?" might have the intent of "Report internet issue"

Training the LLM for Intent Classification: Here's where the power of LLMs comes in. You can train an LLM model on a massive dataset of text conversations and user intents. This dataset should include various phrasings and wording styles that users might employ to express the same intent. TensorFlow provides the framework to train these intent recognition models effectively.

Key Techniques for Intent Recognition:

Pattern Matching: Identify keywords or phrases that typically indicate a specific intent. For example, words like "book," "appointment," or "return" might signify the intent to make a booking or request a return.

Machine Learning Models: Train LLM models to classify user intents based on the overall context and phrasing of the message. This is a more nuanced approach that can handle variations in user language.

Refining Intent Recognition: Continuously monitor and improve your intent recognition model. Analyze user interactions and identify cases where the chatbot misinterpreted the intent. Fine-tune your training data and LLM model to address these shortcomings.

By effectively combining a well-designed conversation flow with powerful LLM-based intent recognition, you can create chatbots that not only engage users in natural conversation but also understand their underlying goals and respond accordingly. The following sections will explore additional aspects of building LLM chatbots, like entity extraction and dialogue generation.

3.2. Training Chatbots with TensorFlow and LLM Techniques

Large Language Models (LLMs) and TensorFlow join forces to create a powerful foundation for training intelligent chatbots. This section dives into how these tools can be used to build chatbots that excel at understanding user intent, generating natural responses, and providing a seamless conversational experience.

1. Leveraging TensorFlow: The Training Playground
TensorFlow provides a robust platform for training the various LLM models that power chatbot functionalities. Here's how TensorFlow comes into play:

Building Intent Recognition Models: We can leverage TensorFlow's machine learning capabilities to train an LLM model for intent recognition. This model analyzes user messages and classifies them based on the underlying intent (e.g., "report an issue," "make a reservation," etc.). TensorFlow offers various pre-built libraries and functionalities to streamline this process.

Entity Extraction with TensorFlow: Beyond intent, chatbots often need to extract specific entities from user messages. Imagine a travel booking scenario where the chatbot needs to identify the destination city and travel dates mentioned by the user. TensorFlow allows you to train LLM models to recognize and extract these entities from user queries.

Dialogue Generation with TensorFlow: Once the intent and entities are identified, the chatbot needs to respond appropriately. Here's where TensorFlow empowers LLM-based dialogue generation. You can train an LLM model on a vast amount of conversation data using TensorFlow. This enables the chatbot to generate natural language responses tailored to the user's intent, the conversation history, and the overall context.

2. Harnessing the Power of LLM Techniques
LLMs bring a unique set of capabilities to the table, making chatbots more intelligent and engaging:

Fine-tuning Pre-trained LLMs: Pre-trained LLM models like GPT-3 or Jurassic-1 Jumbo offer a powerful starting point. By leveraging TensorFlow, you can fine-tune these models on your specific chatbot conversation data. This significantly reduces training time and effort compared to building an LLM from scratch.

Training on Diverse Conversation Data: The quality of your chatbot's responses hinges on the data it's trained on. For effective intent recognition and dialogue generation, use a dataset rich in real-world conversation examples, covering various phrasings, sentence structures, and user intents relevant to your chatbot's domain.

Incorporating Context Awareness: LLMs can be trained to consider the conversation history and context when generating responses. This allows the chatbot to maintain a coherent flow of conversation and avoid repetitive or irrelevant responses.

3. Building a Robust Training Pipeline
Here are some best practices for establishing a robust training pipeline for your LLM chatbot:

Data Preprocessing: Clean and prepare your conversation data before feeding it to the LLM model. This might involve removing irrelevant information, normalizing text, and potentially anonymizing sensitive data.
Data Augmentation (Optional): Artificially expand your dataset by generating variations of existing data points. This helps the LLM model generalize better and handle unforeseen user phrasings.

Model Evaluation and Refinement: Continuously monitor your chatbot's performance and gather user feedback. Analyze cases where the chatbot misinterpreted intent or generated awkward responses. Use this information to further refine your training data and LLM model.

By effectively combining TensorFlow's functionalities with powerful LLM techniques, you can create chatbots that surpass traditional rule-based systems. These intelligent chatbots can understand user intent in a nuanced way, respond with natural language, and provide a more engaging and informative user experience.

The next sections will explore additional considerations for building advanced chatbots, such as integrating dialogue management systems and deploying your chatbot in real-world applications.

3.3. Integrating Chatbots with Real-World Applications

Large Language Models (LLMs) have transformed chatbots from simple scripted interactions to intelligent conversation partners. Now, let's explore how these LLM-powered chatbots can be integrated into various real-world applications, enhancing user experiences and streamlining processes across different industries.

1. Redefining Customer Service
24/7 Availability: LLM chatbots can handle customer inquiries around the clock, freeing up human agents for more complex issues. This improves customer satisfaction and reduces wait times.

Personalized Support: Chatbots can access customer data and past interactions to personalize the support experience. They can recommend relevant products, answer account-specific questions, and even troubleshoot basic technical problems.

Increased Efficiency: Chatbots can handle repetitive tasks like order tracking, appointment scheduling, or basic troubleshooting, freeing up human agents to focus on more complex customer interactions.

2. Streamlining Sales and Marketing
Lead Generation: Chatbots can engage website visitors, answer product-related questions, and qualify leads by collecting user information and preferences. This allows sales teams to focus on nurturing high-quality leads.

Personalized Product Recommendations: Chatbots can analyze user data and recommend products or services tailored to their needs and interests. This can increase conversion rates and boost sales.

Always-on Sales Support: Chatbots can answer basic sales inquiries outside of business hours, providing a seamless customer experience and potentially converting website visitors into leads.

3. Transforming Education and Training
Personalized Learning: Chatbots can offer personalized learning experiences by adapting to a student's pace and

understanding. They can provide practice exercises, answer questions, and offer feedback on assignments.

24/7 Support: Chatbots can act as virtual tutors, providing students with immediate assistance outside of class hours or whenever they encounter difficulties.

Accessibility and Scalability: Chatbots can offer educational resources and support to a large number of students simultaneously, making education more accessible and scalable.

4. Enhancing Healthcare

Patient Support: Chatbots can answer basic medical questions, schedule appointments, and provide reminders for medication intake. This can alleviate pressure on healthcare providers and empower patients to manage their health more effectively.

Mental Health Support: Chatbots can offer basic mental health screenings and provide resources for further support. They can also offer techniques for stress management and emotional well-being.

Appointment Booking and Reminders: Chatbots can streamline appointment booking and send automated reminders to patients, reducing appointment no-shows and improving healthcare efficiency.

5. Additional Applications

The potential applications of LLM chatbots extend far beyond the examples listed above. Here are some additional possibilities:

Travel and Hospitality: Chatbots can assist with booking travel arrangements, provide recommendations for local attractions, and answer questions about amenities.

Banking and Finance: Chatbots can handle basic banking tasks like checking account balances, transferring funds, and answering questions about financial products.

Government Services: Chatbots can provide information about government programs, answer frequently asked questions, and even schedule appointments for citizens.

By integrating LLM chatbots into these real-world applications, businesses, organizations, and institutions can improve efficiency, enhance customer or user experience, and provide valuable services in a more accessible and interactive way. As LLM technology continues to evolve, we can expect even more innovative applications for chatbots to emerge in the future.

IV. Creating Powerful Summarizers

Large Language Models (LLMs) are revolutionizing the way we process information. One exciting application is the creation of powerful text summarizers. This section explores how LLMs can be harnessed to condense lengthy pieces of text into informative and concise summaries, saving you valuable time and effort.

1. Why Summarization Matters in the Age of Information Overload
In today's digital world, we're bombarded with information. From news articles to research papers, the sheer volume of text can be overwhelming. Text summarization offers a solution:

Improved Information Consumption: Effective summaries allow you to grasp the main points of a text quickly, deciding whether it's worth reading in its entirety.

Enhanced Research Efficiency: Summarization tools can help researchers quickly scan through large amounts of literature to identify relevant studies and key findings.
Streamlined Content Creation: Summaries can provide a concise overview of a topic, serving as a springboard for further content creation or analysis.

2. Unveiling the Techniques Behind LLM Summarization

LLMs bring a unique approach to text summarization, going beyond simple keyword extraction:

Extractive Summarization: This traditional approach identifies the most important sentences from the text and combines them to form a summary. LLMs excel at this by analyzing sentence structure, word importance, and overall content relevance.

Abstractive Summarization: This method goes a step further. LLMs not only pick key sentences but also rephrase and rewrite them to create a new, concise summary that captures the essence of the original text. This requires a deeper understanding of the text's meaning and context.

3. Empowering Summarizers with LLM Capabilities
LLMs possess several key strengths that make them powerful tools for summarization:

Understanding Context and Semantics: LLMs can go beyond surface-level analysis to grasp the underlying meaning and relationships between words and sentences. This allows them to identify the most important information and generate summaries that are both accurate and informative.

Extractive and Abstractive Summarization: As discussed earlier, LLMs can handle both extractive summarization (selecting key sentences) and abstractive summarization (generating new text). This versatility allows you to choose the summarization approach that best suits your needs.

Adaptability to Different Text Formats: LLMs can be trained on various text formats, from news articles and research papers to emails and social media posts. This makes them adaptable to a wide range of summarization tasks.

4. Building and Training LLM Summarizers
Here's a glimpse into the process of building and training LLM summarizers:

Data Preparation: Large datasets of text documents and their corresponding human-written summaries are essential for training. This data provides a benchmark for the LLM to learn how to identify important information and generate concise summaries.

Model Selection and Training: Choosing the right LLM architecture and training it on the prepared data is crucial. Popular options include transformer-based models like BART or T5, specifically designed for text summarization tasks.

Fine-tuning for Specific Domains: For optimal performance, consider fine-tuning your LLM model on domain-specific data. For example, a summarizer for medical research papers might benefit from fine-tuning on a dataset of medical literature and summaries.
5. Utilizing Summarization Tools in Action

LLM-powered summarizers offer a variety of practical applications:

News Aggregators: Summarization tools can condense news articles and provide quick overviews of current events, allowing users to stay informed without getting bogged down in lengthy articles.

Research Assistants: Researchers can use summarization tools to quickly scan through large volumes of academic literature, identifying relevant studies and key findings.

Content Creation: Summarizers can generate concise summaries of longer pieces of content, providing a starting point for blog posts, articles, or other content formats.

Accessibility Tools: Text summarization can be a valuable tool for people with reading difficulties, allowing them to access and understand complex information.

As LLM technology continues to evolve, text summarization tools will become even more sophisticated and versatile. These tools have the potential to revolutionize the way we interact with information, allowing us to process and understand vast amounts of text with greater efficiency and clarity.

4.1. Extractive vs. Abstractive Summarization Techniques

In the age of information overload, text summarization has become a valuable tool. Large Language Models (LLMs) are at the forefront of this field, offering two primary summarization techniques: extractive and abstractive. Here, we'll delve into the distinctions between these approaches, exploring their strengths and weaknesses to help you choose the right method for your needs.

1. Extractive Summarization: A Focus on Key Sentences
Imagine a highlighter that intelligently selects the most important sentences in a document. That's the essence of extractive summarization. This technique identifies and extracts salient sentences from the original text to create a concise summary.

Core Function: Extractive summarization algorithms analyze the text for factors like sentence position, word frequency, and word importance. Based on this analysis, they select the sentences believed to convey the most critical information in the document.

Advantages:

Accuracy: Extractive summarization is generally reliable for factual texts where key information is explicitly stated.

Efficiency: This approach is computationally less expensive compared to abstractive summarization.
Fidelity to Source: Extractive summaries tend to maintain the original wording and sentence structure, ensuring factual accuracy.

Disadvantages:

Limited Creativity: Extractive summaries simply combine existing sentences, lacking the ability to rephrase or synthesize information.

Redundancy: The extracted sentences might contain some overlap or redundancy, leading to a less polished summary.
Difficulty Capturing Complexities: For nuanced or elaborate texts, extractive summaries might struggle to capture the full depth of meaning.

2. Abstractive Summarization: Rethinking and Rewriting
Extractive summarization highlights existing sentences, while abstractive summarization takes a bolder approach. This technique involves not just selecting sentences but also understanding the overall context and meaning of the text. The LLM then rephrases and

condenses the information to create a new, concise summary.

Core Function: Abstractive summarization utilizes LLMs' ability to grasp semantics and relationships between words. The model analyzes the text, identifies key points, and then generates a new summary that conveys the essential meaning in a concise and potentially rephrased way.

Advantages:

Informative and Concise: Abstractive summaries can capture the essence of the text in a more natural and readable way, often using fewer words than the original text.

Creativity and Flow: LLMs can rephrase and synthesize information, leading to summaries with better flow and readability.

Handling Complex Texts: Abstractive summarization is well-suited for nuanced or intricate texts where capturing the overall meaning is crucial.
Disadvantages:

Accuracy Challenges: There's a higher risk of factual errors, especially for complex topics, as the LLM rephrases and condenses information.

Computational Cost: Training and running abstractive summarization models requires more computational resources compared to extractive techniques.

Potential for Bias: LLMs can inherit biases from their training data, which might be reflected in the generated summaries.

3. Choosing the Right Technique: It Depends on Your Needs

When deciding between extractive and abstractive summarization, consider these factors:

Type of Text: For factual texts with explicitly stated key points, extractive summarization might be sufficient. For more complex or nuanced texts, abstractive summarization can provide a better understanding.

Desired Outcome: If factual accuracy is paramount, extractive summarization is a safer choice. If readability, conciseness, and capturing the overall essence are your priorities, abstractive summarization might be preferable.

Available Resources: Extractive summarization is generally less computationally expensive. If computational resources are limited, it might be the more practical option.

Both extractive and abstractive summarization techniques have their strengths and weaknesses. By understanding these distinctions and considering your specific needs, you can choose the most appropriate approach to generate informative and concise summaries that effectively convey the essence of the original text.

4.2. Fine-tuning Pre-trained LLMs for Summarization Tasks

Large Language Models (LLMs) are revolutionizing text summarization. However, their true potential is unlocked through fine-tuning, a process that tailors these powerful models for specific tasks like summarization. This section explores how fine-tuning pre-trained LLMs empowers them to excel at generating informative and concise summaries.

1. The Advantages of Pre-trained LLMs for Summarization

Pre-trained LLMs like BART or T5 offer a strong foundation for building effective summarization systems. Here's why they are a good starting point:

Extensive Knowledge Base: Pre-trained LLMs are trained on massive amounts of text data, giving them a vast understanding of language structure, semantics, and relationships between words. This knowledge base proves invaluable for tasks like summarization, where comprehending the context and meaning of text is crucial.

Transfer Learning Efficiency: Fine-tuning leverages the pre-trained knowledge of the LLM as a starting point. This significantly reduces training time and computational resources compared to building a summarization model from scratch.

Adaptability to Different Domains: Many pre-trained LLMs are designed to handle various text formats. Fine-tuning allows you to specialize the model for a specific domain, such as news articles, scientific papers, or legal documents.

2. Unveiling the Fine-Tuning Process
Fine-tuning bridges the gap between a general-purpose LLM and a task-specific summarization model. Here's a breakdown of the key steps:

Data Preparation: Gather a high-quality dataset of text documents and their corresponding human-written summaries. This dataset provides the foundation for the LLM to learn how to identify important information and generate concise summaries.

Model Selection: Choose a pre-trained LLM architecture specifically designed for text summarization tasks, like BART or T5. These models often have built-in mechanisms for handling encoder-decoder tasks, essential for summarization.
Training with Fine-tuning: The pre-trained LLM is not entirely retrained. Instead, specific layers or parameters are adjusted based on the summarization dataset. This

refines the model's ability to identify key information and generate summaries relevant to the specific task.

3. Optimizing Fine-tuning for Summarization Performance

Here are some additional considerations to maximize the effectiveness of fine-tuning for summarization:

Choosing the Right Hyperparameters: Hyperparameters control the learning process of the LLM. Experimenting with different learning rates, batch sizes, and optimizer configurations can significantly impact the quality of the generated summaries.

Data Augmentation Techniques: Artificially expanding your dataset with variations of existing examples (e.g., paraphrasing sentences, shortening summaries) can help the LLM generalize better and handle unseen text patterns.

Evaluation Metrics: Go beyond simple accuracy metrics. Use ROUGE scores, which compare the generated summary to human-written summaries, to assess the quality and factual correctness of the summaries.

4. Unveiling the Benefits of Fine-tuned Summarization Systems

Fine-tuned LLMs offer several advantages for text summarization tasks:

Improved Accuracy and Informativeness: Fine-tuned models can identify key information more effectively and generate summaries that accurately capture the essence of the original text.

Enhanced Readability and Conciseness: The summarization process condenses the information while maintaining clarity and flow, making it easier for users to grasp the main points.

Domain-Specific Expertise: Fine-tuning on domain-specific data allows the LLM to tailor its summaries to incorporate relevant terminology and concepts, leading to more meaningful summaries for users in that domain.

5. The Future of Fine-tuned Summarization Systems

As LLM technology advances and access to computational resources increases, fine-tuned summarization systems will become even more sophisticated. Here are some exciting possibilities:

Real-time Summarization: Imagine being able to get summaries of news articles, research papers, or even lengthy emails in real-time. Fine-tuned LLMs have the potential to make this a reality.

Summarization with Multiple Styles: Fine-tuning could allow for generating summaries tailored to different audiences or purposes. For instance, a summary for a technical report might be more detailed than one for a news article.

Multilingual Summarization: Fine-tuning LMs on multilingual data could break down language barriers and allow for summaries of text in different languages.

By leveraging the power of pre-trained LLMs and fine-tuning them for specific summarization tasks, we can unlock a new level of efficiency and understanding in our interactions with information.

4.3. Evaluating and Improving Summarization Performance

Crafting effective text summarization systems hinges on the ability to measure their performance and identify areas for improvement. This section explores various techniques for evaluating summarization models and strategies to refine them for generating informative and concise summaries.

1. Why Evaluation Matters in Summarization

Evaluating your summarization system goes beyond simply reading the generated summaries. Here's why a robust evaluation process is crucial:

Identifying Strengths and Weaknesses: Evaluation metrics help pinpoint areas where your model excels and areas that need improvement. This allows you to

focus your efforts on refining specific aspects of the model.
Comparing Different Models: Evaluation metrics provide a common ground for comparing the performance of different summarization models. This is essential for choosing the best model for your specific needs.

Tracking Progress Over Time: Regular evaluation allows you to monitor the effectiveness of your summarization system over time, especially after implementing improvements or fine-tuning the model.

2. Beyond Accuracy: A Look at Popular Evaluation Metrics
While accuracy is important, it's not the sole metric for evaluating summarization systems. Here are some key metrics to consider:

ROUGE Scores (Recall-Oriented Understudy for Gisting Evaluation): A suite of metrics that compare the overlap between machine-generated summaries and human-written reference summaries. ROUGE scores consider different aspects of overlap, such as n-grams (sequences of words) and longest common subsequences.

BLEU (Bi-Lingual Evaluation Understudy): Another metric that measures n-gram overlap between generated summaries and reference summaries. However, BLEU is less effective than ROUGE scores for evaluating summaries in languages other than English.

Human Evaluation: While time-consuming, human evaluation remains a valuable tool. Human evaluators can assess the overall quality, readability, and informativeness of the summaries, which might not be fully captured by automatic metrics.

3. Strategies to Enhance Summarization Performance
Once you've evaluated your model, here are some strategies to address shortcomings and improve its performance:

Data Quality and Augmentation: The quality of your training data significantly impacts the effectiveness of your model. Ensure your data is diverse, accurate, and relevant to the summarization task. Consider data augmentation techniques like paraphrasing sentences or shortening summaries to improve the model's generalization ability.

Hyperparameter Tuning: Fine-tuning hyperparameters like learning rates, batch sizes, and optimizer configurations can significantly improve the model's ability to identify key information and generate concise summaries. Experiment with different settings to find the optimal configuration for your specific task.

Model Selection and Fine-tuning: Choosing the right pre-trained LLM architecture and fine-tuning it effectively are crucial. Explore different LLM models specifically designed for summarization tasks, such as BART or T5. Fine-tuning these models on your domain-specific data can significantly enhance performance compared to generic models.

Ensemble Learning: Consider combining multiple summarization models with different strengths. This ensemble approach can often outperform individual models by leveraging the unique capabilities of each system.

4. The Road Ahead: Future Directions in Summarization Evaluation

As LLM technology advances, so too will the methods for evaluating summarization performance. Here are some emerging trends:

Moving Beyond ROUGE Scores: While ROUGE scores offer valuable insights, they have limitations. Researchers are exploring alternative metrics that consider factors like factual correctness, summarization style, and semantic similarity to human-written summaries.

Human-in-the-Loop Evaluation: Integrating human feedback into the evaluation process can provide valuable insights for further refinement. This might involve human evaluators providing ratings or corrections to machine-generated summaries.

Evaluating User Experience: Ultimately, the goal of summarization is to enhance user experience. Future evaluation methods might incorporate user studies to assess how well summaries meet user needs and improve information comprehension.

By employing a comprehensive evaluation strategy and continuously refining your summarization system, you can ensure it delivers informative, concise, and valuable summaries that empower users to grasp the essence of text in a more efficient and effective way.

,

V. Exploring Advanced LLM Applications

Large Language Models (LLMs) are rapidly evolving, pushing the boundaries of what's possible in the realm of artificial intelligence. Beyond well-established applications like chatbots and text summarization, LLMs are venturing into exciting new territories. Here, we'll delve into some of the most promising advanced LLM applications that are shaping the future:

1. Redefining Creativity: LLMs as Artistic Partners

Generating Different Creative Text Formats: LLMs can create poems, scripts, musical pieces, and even computer code in various styles, partnering with human creators to spark new ideas and explore diverse creative avenues.

Personalized Content Creation: Imagine an LLM that tailors content to your specific style and preferences. This could involve generating marketing copy that resonates with your target audience or crafting blog posts that reflect your unique voice.
Bridging the Language Gap: LLMs can translate creative text formats like poems or song lyrics while preserving the essence and artistic intent of the original work. This

opens doors for broader cultural exchange and appreciation.

2. Reimagining Code: AI-powered Programming

Code Completion and Generation: LLMs can assist programmers by automatically completing code snippets, suggesting alternative approaches, or even generating basic code structures based on natural language descriptions.
Identifying and Fixing Bugs: LLMs can analyze code to detect potential bugs and vulnerabilities, streamlining the software development process.
Translating between Programming Languages: LLMs hold promise for translating code between different programming languages, simplifying collaboration and knowledge sharing across development teams.

3. Scientific Discovery and Exploration

Literature Reviews and Knowledge Synthesis: LLMs can analyze vast amounts of scientific literature, identifying research trends, summarizing key findings, and assisting researchers in navigating complex scientific domains.
Hypothesis Generation and Experiment Design: LLMs can analyze existing data and scientific knowledge to propose new hypotheses and suggest potential experimental designs to test them, accelerating scientific discovery.
Drug Discovery and Material Science: LLMs can be used to analyze molecular structures and predict their

properties, aiding in the development of new drugs and materials.

4. Rethinking Human-Computer Interaction

Natural Language Interfaces (NLIs): LLMs can power advanced NLIs that allow users to interact with computers and devices using natural language, making technology more accessible and intuitive for everyone.

Personalized User Experiences: LLMs can personalize user experiences across various platforms, tailoring content recommendations, search results, and even educational materials to individual user preferences and learning styles.

Real-time Translation and Communication: LLMs can enable seamless real-time translation between languages, fostering communication and collaboration across cultures and geographical boundaries.

5. The Future Landscape: Emerging Applications

As LLM technology continues to evolve, we can expect even more groundbreaking applications to emerge:

Combating Misinformation and Bias: LLMs can be trained to identify and flag potentially misleading information online, contributing to a more informed and trustworthy digital environment.

Personalized Education and Learning: LLMs can create personalized learning pathways, adapting to individual student needs and learning styles, enhancing the effectiveness of education systems.

Augmented Reality and Virtual Reality Experiences: LLMs can create dynamic and interactive experiences in AR/VR environments, by generating realistic dialogue for virtual characters or crafting immersive narratives.

The potential applications of LLMs are vast and constantly expanding. As we continue to explore and refine these technologies, we can expect them to play an increasingly transformative role in various aspects of our lives, from enhancing creativity and scientific discovery to revolutionizing the way we interact with technology and information.

5.1. Text Generation Beyond Chatbots: Machine Translation, Creative Writing

Large Language Models (LLMs) are revolutionizing text generation, venturing far beyond the realm of chatbots. Their ability to understand and process language empowers them to generate creative text formats, translate languages with nuance, and even weave tales that spark the imagination.

1. Unleashing Creativity: LLMs as Artistic Collaborators
LLMs are transforming how we approach creative writing and content generation:

Generating Different Creative Text Formats: Imagine an LLM that can compose poems in the style of your favorite poet or craft a compelling movie script brimming with witty dialogue. LLMs can generate various creative text formats, acting as a springboard for human creativity or even co-creating alongside writers.

Personalized Content Creation: Writer's block? LLMs can help! They can generate marketing copy tailored to a specific audience or create blog posts that reflect your unique voice and style. This allows creators to focus on refining ideas and adding their personal touch.

Bridging the Language Gap: LLMs can translate creative text formats like poems or song lyrics, ensuring the essence and artistic intent of the original work are preserved. This paves the way for broader cultural exchange and appreciation of diverse creative expressions.

2. Breaking Language Barriers: Machine Translation with Nuance

Machine translation has come a long way, and LLMs are pushing the boundaries even further:

Moving Beyond Literal Translations: LLMs can translate with a deeper understanding of context and nuance. They can capture the intended meaning and emotional tone of the original text, resulting in more natural-sounding and accurate translations.

Preserving Style and Creativity: When translating creative text formats like poems or scripts, LLMs can strive to maintain the original style and artistic voice. This is crucial for conveying the full impact of the creative work in a new language.

Multilingual Communication Made Easy: LLMs hold the potential to enable real-time translation conversations, fostering seamless communication and collaboration across cultures and languages. Imagine having an LLM that can translate a business meeting or a casual conversation on the fly, breaking down language barriers and promoting global understanding.

3. The Future of Text Generation: Where are We Headed?
As LLM technology continues to evolve, we can expect even more exciting possibilities in text generation:

Combating Misinformation and Bias: LLMs can be trained to identify potentially misleading information and translate it with appropriate context or disclaimers, contributing to a more trustworthy online environment.
Personalized Education and Learning: Imagine educational materials that adapt to your learning style and native language. LLMs can personalize learning experiences by translating and generating content that caters to individual needs.

Augmented Reality and Virtual Reality Experiences: LLMs can craft dynamic and interactive narratives for AR/VR environments. They can generate realistic dialogue for virtual characters or create immersive storylines that transport users to fantastical worlds.

The potential of LLMs in text generation is vast and brimming with possibilities. As we continue to develop and refine these technologies, they have the potential to revolutionize the way we create, translate, and consume information, fostering a more connected and creatively rich world.

5.2. Leveraging LLMs for Question Answering Systems

Large Language Models (LLMs) are revolutionizing the way we interact with information. One exciting application is their use in building powerful question answering (QA) systems. This section explores how LLMs can be leveraged to create intelligent systems that can effectively answer user queries, spanning factual topics to open ended, challenging questions.

1. Why LLMs Are Ideal for Next-Gen QA Systems
Traditional QA systems often rely on keyword matching and retrieval techniques, which can be limiting. LLMs offer several advantages:

Deeper Understanding of Language: LLMs go beyond surface-level analysis. They can grasp the context and meaning behind a question, allowing them to identify the most relevant information even if it's not explicitly stated using the exact keywords.

Answering Open Ended Questions: LLMs can handle complex or open ended questions that require reasoning and inference. They can analyze vast amounts of information, identify relationships between concepts, and generate thoughtful answers that go beyond simple factual retrieval.

Adaptability to Different Domains: LLMs can be trained on domain-specific data, enabling them to answer questions about specific fields like medicine, law, or engineering with greater accuracy and understanding of the relevant terminology and concepts.

2. Unveiling the Techniques: How LLMs Power QA Systems

LLMs can be employed in various ways to create intelligent QA systems:

Extractive Question Answering: Here, LLMs identify the most relevant answer passages from a document or knowledge base. They analyze the question and the text, pinpointing sections that contain the information needed to answer the question accurately.

Abstractive Question Answering: This approach goes a step further. LLMs not only find relevant passages but also paraphrase, summarize, and synthesize the information to generate a concise and informative answer directly, without relying on copying text from the source.

Generative Question Answering: For open ended, challenging, or opinion-based questions, LLMs can leverage their knowledge and understanding of the world to generate thoughtful and informative answers, even if there's no single definitive answer available.

3. Building Effective LLM-powered QA Systems
Here are some key considerations for building robust QA systems with LLMs:

Data Preparation: High-quality training data is crucial. This includes question-answer pairs spanning various formats and domains, depending on the intended use case of the QA system.

Model Selection and Training: Choosing the right LLM architecture and training it effectively is essential. Models like BART or T5, designed for text summarization and question answering tasks, can be strong starting points.

Evaluation and Refinement: Continuously evaluate the performance of your QA system using relevant metrics. This allows you to identify areas for improvement and refine the LLM through techniques like fine-tuning or adjusting training parameters.

4. The Future of LLM-powered QA Systems
As LLM technology advances, we can expect even more sophisticated QA systems:

Real-time Question Answering: Imagine being able to ask questions and receive answers in real-time, no matter where you are. LLMs have the potential to power intelligent assistants that can answer your questions on the fly, using information from the web or your personal data.

Context-aware Question Answering: QA systems will become more adept at understanding the context of a question. They will consider the user's past interactions, current location, and search history to provide the most relevant and helpful answers.

Explainable AI: Transparency and trust are crucial. Future QA systems might incorporate functionalities that explain how the LLM arrived at an answer, allowing users to understand the reasoning behind the response.

By leveraging the power of LLMs, we can build intelligent QA systems that empower users to access information more effectively, regardless of the complexity of their questions. These systems have the potential to transform the way we interact with information, fostering a future of lifelong learning and knowledge discovery.

5.3. Building Custom LLM Applications with TensorFlow

Large Language Models (LLMs) are revolutionizing various fields, and TensorFlow provides a powerful toolkit for building custom LLM applications. This section explores the steps involved in creating and deploying LLMs using TensorFlow, empowering you to harness the potential of these intelligent models for your specific needs.

1. Setting the Stage: Prerequisites for Building LLM Applications
Before diving into code, ensure you have the essential building blocks:

TensorFlow Environment: Install TensorFlow on your system, ensuring compatibility with your hardware (CPU, GPU) and chosen programming language (Python is common).

LLM Selection: Choose a pre-trained LLM architecture suitable for your task. Popular options include BART for text summarization or T5 for general-purpose text-to-text tasks.
Task Definition: Clearly define the problem you want your LLM application to solve. This will guide your data preparation and model selection.

2. Data Preparation: The Foundation of Effective LLMs
LLMs thrive on high-quality data. Here's how to prepare your data for building custom LLM applications:

Data Collection: Gather a dataset relevant to your task. This might involve text documents, code snippets, question-answer pairs, or any other format suited to your chosen LLM architecture.

Data Preprocessing: Clean and pre-process your data. This includes removing irrelevant information, formatting text consistently (e.g., lowercase conversion), and potentially tokenizing the text into sequences of words or characters.

Data Splitting: Divide your data into training, validation, and test sets. The training set is used to train the LLM, the validation set helps fine-tune hyperparameters, and the test set evaluates the final model's performance.

3. Building Your LLM Application with TensorFlow
TensorFlow offers various tools to construct and train your LLM application:

Keras API: A high-level API within TensorFlow that simplifies model building. Leverage pre-built LLM architectures from TensorFlow Hub or Keras applications like BART or T5 as a foundation for your custom model.
Model Customization: While using a pre-trained LLM as a starting point, you can customize layers or

hyperparameters (learning rate, optimizer) to fine-tune the model for your specific task and data.

Training and Evaluation: Train your LLM using the prepared data. Monitor training progress on the validation set and adjust hyperparameters as needed. Once training is complete, evaluate the model's performance on the test set using relevant metrics.

4. Deployment Considerations: Sharing Your LLM Application

Once you've built and trained your LLM application, consider how you want to deploy it:

TensorFlow Serving: A framework for serving TensorFlow models. Package your trained LLM model for production and deploy it using TensorFlow Serving, allowing users to interact with your model through APIs. Cloud Deployment: Consider cloud platforms like Google Cloud AI Platform that offer pre-built infrastructure for deploying and managing machine learning models, simplifying the deployment process.

5. Beyond the Basics: Advanced Techniques for LLM Applications

As you explore building more sophisticated LLM applications, consider these advanced techniques:

Transfer Learning: Fine-tune a pre-trained LLM on a smaller dataset specific to your task. This can significantly improve performance compared to training from scratch, especially for tasks with limited data.

Multi-task Learning: Train your LLM on multiple related tasks simultaneously. This can improve performance on all tasks by allowing the model to learn shared representations between them.

Ensemble Learning: Combine multiple LLM models with different strengths to create an ensemble model that often outperforms individual models.

6. Conclusion: The Potential of Custom LLM Applications

Building custom LLM applications with TensorFlow opens doors to a vast array of possibilities. By following these steps and exploring advanced techniques, you can leverage the power of LLMs to solve real-world problems and create innovative applications in various fields, from text summarization and question answering to code generation and creative writing. As LLM technology continues to evolve, the potential for custom applications will only grow, shaping the future of artificial intelligence and human-computer interaction.

VI. Mastering TensorFlow for LLM Development

Large Language Models (LLMs) are revolutionizing numerous fields, and TensorFlow stands as a powerful toolkit for crafting custom LLM applications. This comprehensive guide explores the journey of mastering TensorFlow for LLM development, equipping you with the knowledge and skills to harness the potential of these intelligent models.

1. Building a Strong Foundation: Prerequisites and Knowledge
Before embarking on your TensorFlow and LLM adventure, ensure you have a solid foundation in place:

TensorFlow Expertise: Gain proficiency in TensorFlow. This includes understanding core concepts like tensors, data pipelines, and building models using the Keras API. Numerous online tutorials, courses, and the official TensorFlow documentation can be valuable resources.
Machine Learning Fundamentals: Grasp fundamental machine learning concepts like supervised learning, loss functions, optimizers, and evaluation metrics. These concepts are crucial for training and evaluating your LLM models effectively.

Programming Proficiency: A strong foundation in Python programming is essential. Python is the primary language used with TensorFlow, and familiarity with libraries like NumPy and Pandas will further enhance your development experience.

2. Unveiling the LLM Landscape: Architectures and Applications
Familiarize yourself with the world of LLMs:

Popular LLM Architectures: Explore prominent LLM architectures like transformers, specifically models like BART (for text summarization) or T5 (for general-purpose text-to-text tasks). Understanding their strengths and functionalities will guide your choice for your custom application.

Real-World LLM Applications: Gain inspiration from existing LLM applications like text summarization tools, chatbots, or code generation systems. This will spark ideas for your own LLM project and provide context for the capabilities you can build.

3. Data Preparation: The Fuel for Effective LLMs
High-quality data is the lifeblood of successful LLM development. Here's how to prepare your data for TensorFlow and LLMs:

Data Collection: Gather a dataset relevant to your chosen LLM application. This might involve text documents, code snippets, question-answer pairs, or any other format suited to your specific task.

Data Preprocessing: Clean and pre-process your data meticulously. This includes removing irrelevant information, formatting text consistently, and potentially tokenizing the text into sequences of words or characters. Tools like TensorFlow Text can simplify this process.

Data Augmentation (Optional): Consider data augmentation techniques to improve the robustness of your model. This might involve techniques like synonym replacement, back-translation (for multilingual tasks), or text paraphrasing.

4. Constructing Your LLM Application with TensorFlow
TensorFlow offers a powerful suite of tools to bring your LLM application to life:

Leveraging Pre-trained Models: Take advantage of pre-trained LLM models from TensorFlow Hub. These models can serve as a robust starting point, reducing training time and effort.

Keras API for Model Building: Utilize the Keras API within TensorFlow for building and customizing your LLM application. Keras provides a high-level interface that simplifies the model creation process.

Fine-tuning for Your Task: While using a pre-trained model as a foundation, fine-tune specific layers or hyperparameters (learning rate, optimizer) to optimize the model's performance for your specific task and data.

5. Training and Evaluation: Refining Your LLM
The training and evaluation phase is crucial for creating an effective LLM application:

Training with TensorFlow: Train your LLM model using the prepared data and TensorFlow. Monitor training progress closely, paying attention to metrics like loss and accuracy. Utilize techniques like early stopping to prevent overfitting.

Evaluation Strategies: Go beyond basic accuracy metrics. Consider using task-specific evaluation metrics like ROUGE scores (for summarization) or BLEU scores (for machine translation) to assess the quality and relevance of your model's outputs.

Visualization Techniques: Employ visualization tools like TensorBoard to visualize training progress, track key metrics, and identify potential issues with your model's learning process.

6. Deployment Considerations: Sharing Your LLM Creation

Once your LLM application is trained and evaluated, consider how you want to share it with the world:

TensorFlow Serving: Package your trained model for production and deploy it using TensorFlow Serving. This allows users to interact with your model through APIs, enabling real-world applications.

Cloud Platforms: Explore cloud platforms like Google Cloud AI Platform that offer pre-built infrastructure for deploying and managing machine learning models. These platforms can simplify the deployment process and provide scalability.

7. Deepening Your Expertise: Advanced Techniques for LLMs

Having mastered the fundamentals of building LLM applications with TensorFlow, it's time to delve into advanced techniques that will push the boundaries of your creations. This section equips you with powerful tools to enhance your LLM development journey.

1. Transfer Learning: Leveraging Pre-trained Knowledge While pre-trained LLMs offer a strong foundation, transfer learning unlocks their true potential for custom applications. Here's how:

Fine-tuning: This technique involves taking a pre-trained LLM like BART or T5 and adjusting specific layers or hyperparameters. You train the model on your smaller, task-specific dataset, allowing it to leverage its pre-existing knowledge while adapting to your unique requirements. This is particularly beneficial for tasks with limited data, where training from scratch might be impractical.

Advantages of Transfer Learning:

Faster Training: By leveraging pre-trained knowledge, transfer learning significantly reduces training time compared to training a model from scratch.
Improved Performance: Fine-tuning a pre-trained LLM often leads to better performance on your specific task

compared to training a new model from scratch, especially for complex tasks.

Example: Imagine you're building a custom LLM for code generation. You can fine-tune a pre-trained LLM on a massive code dataset, then further refine it on your specific programming language or coding domain.

2. Multi-task Learning: Training for Multiple Tasks Simultaneously

Multi-task learning allows you to train your LLM on multiple related tasks concurrently. This can be particularly beneficial if the tasks share underlying similarities. Here's the concept:

Shared Representations: By training on multiple tasks simultaneously, the LLM learns to identify shared representations between the tasks. This improves performance on all tasks compared to training separate models for each individual task.

Example: You're building an LLM for a virtual assistant that needs to handle tasks like summarizing news articles, writing emails, and generating creative text formats. By training the LLM on all these tasks simultaneously through multi-tasking learning, it can learn the nuances of language that are generally applicable across these domains, leading to better performance on each individual task.

3. Ensemble Learning: Combining Strengths for Superior Performance

Ensemble learning involves combining multiple LLM models with different strengths to create an even more powerful model. Here's the strategy:

Harnessing Diversity: Each LLM model in the ensemble might be trained on different data, with different architectures, or using different hyperparameters. This diversity in training approaches leads to a more robust ensemble model.

Combining Outputs: There are various techniques to combine the outputs from the different models within the ensemble. Averaging predictions or using weighted voting are common approaches.

Benefits of Ensemble Learning:

Improved Accuracy: Ensemble models often outperform individual models by leveraging the unique strengths of each component model.
Reduced Variance: Ensembles can help reduce the variance of the model's predictions, leading to more consistent and reliable outputs.
Example: You can create an ensemble of LLMs trained with different summarization techniques (e.g., abstractive vs. extractive) to generate more comprehensive and informative summaries.

4. Prompt Engineering: The Art of Guiding LLMs

Prompt engineering plays a crucial role in guiding LLMs towards generating the desired outputs. Here's how to master this art:

Crafting Effective Prompts: Effective prompts are clear, concise, and informative. They communicate your intent to the LLM by providing context, specifying the desired task, and offering examples. The quality of your prompts significantly influences the quality and relevance of the model's responses.

Prompt Engineering Techniques:

Instructional Prompts: Clearly state the task you want the LLM to perform (e.g., "Write a poem in the style of Shakespeare").

Informative Prompts: Provide relevant background information or context to guide the LLM (e.g., "Write a news article summarizing the latest scientific discovery about climate change").

Few-Shot Learning Prompts: Provide a few examples of the desired output format to help the LLM understand the style and structure (e.g., "Here are some examples of code comments, write similar comments for this new code block").

Example: By carefully crafting prompts, you can guide your LLM to generate different creative text formats like poems, code snippets, or musical pieces.

By mastering these advanced techniques, you can unlock the full potential of LLMs and create powerful custom applications that address real-world challenges.

Remember, this is an ongoing field of exploration. Keep yourself updated with the latest advancements in transfer learning, multi-task learning, ensemble methods, and prompt engineering to stay ahead of the curve in LLM development.

VI. Mastering TensorFlow for LLM Development

Large Language Models (LLMs) are revolutionizing various fields, and TensorFlow stands as a powerful toolkit for crafting custom LLM applications. This comprehensive guide explores the journey of mastering TensorFlow for LLM development, equipping you with the knowledge and skills to harness the potential of these intelligent models.

1. Building a Strong Foundation: Prerequisites and Knowledge
Before embarking on your TensorFlow and LLM adventure, ensure you have a solid foundation in place:

TensorFlow Expertise: Gain proficiency in TensorFlow. This includes understanding core concepts like tensors, data pipelines, and building models using the Keras API. Numerous online tutorials, courses, and the official TensorFlow documentation can be valuable resources.
Machine Learning Fundamentals: Grasp fundamental machine learning concepts like supervised learning, loss functions, optimizers, and evaluation metrics. These concepts are crucial for training and evaluating your LLM models effectively.

Programming Proficiency: A strong foundation in Python programming is essential. Python is the primary language used with TensorFlow, and familiarity with libraries like NumPy and Pandas will further enhance your development experience.

2. Unveiling the LLM Landscape: Architectures and Applications
Familiarize yourself with the world of LLMs:

Popular LLM Architectures: Explore prominent LLM architectures like transformers, specifically models like BART (for text summarization) or T5 (for general-purpose text-to-text tasks). Understanding their strengths and functionalities will guide your choice for your custom application.

Real-World LLM Applications: Gain inspiration from existing LLM applications like text summarization tools, chatbots, or code generation systems. This will spark ideas for your own LLM project and provide context for the capabilities you can build.

3. Data Preparation: The Fuel for Effective LLMs
High-quality data is the lifeblood of successful LLM development. Here's how to prepare your data for TensorFlow and LLMs:

Data Collection: Gather a dataset relevant to your chosen LLM application. This might involve text documents, code snippets, question-answer pairs, or any other format suited to your specific task.

Data Preprocessing: Clean and pre-process your data meticulously. This includes removing irrelevant information, formatting text consistently (e.g., lowercase conversion), and potentially tokenizing the text into sequences of words or characters. Tools like TensorFlow Text can simplify this process.

Data Augmentation (Optional): Consider data augmentation techniques to improve the robustness of your model. This might involve techniques like synonym replacement, back-translation (for multilingual tasks), or text paraphrasing.

4. Constructing Your LLM Application with TensorFlow
TensorFlow offers a powerful suite of tools to bring your LLM application to life:

Leveraging Pre-trained Models: Take advantage of pre-trained LLM models from TensorFlow Hub. These models can serve as a robust starting point, reducing training time and effort.

Keras API for Model Building: Utilize the Keras API within TensorFlow for building and customizing your LLM application. Keras provides a high-level interface that simplifies the model creation process.

Fine-tuning for Your Task: While using a pre-trained model as a foundation, fine-tune specific layers or hyperparameters (learning rate, optimizer) to optimize the model's performance for your specific task and data.

5. Training and Evaluation: Refining Your LLM
The training and evaluation phase is crucial for creating an effective LLM application:

Training with TensorFlow: Train your LLM model using the prepared data and TensorFlow. Monitor training progress closely, paying attention to metrics like loss and accuracy. Utilize techniques like early stopping to prevent overfitting.

Evaluation Strategies: Go beyond basic accuracy metrics. Consider using task-specific evaluation metrics like ROUGE scores (for summarization) or BLEU scores (for machine translation) to assess the quality and relevance of your model's outputs.

Visualization Techniques: Employ visualization tools like TensorBoard to visualize training progress, track key metrics, and identify potential issues with your model's learning process.

6. Deployment Considerations: Sharing Your LLM Creation

Once your LLM application is trained and evaluated, consider how you want to share it with the world:

TensorFlow Serving: Package your trained model for production and deploy it using TensorFlow Serving. This allows users to interact with your model through APIs, enabling real-world applications.

Cloud Platforms: Explore cloud platforms like Google Cloud AI Platform that offer pre-built infrastructure for deploying and managing machine learning models. These platforms can simplify the deployment process and provide scalability.

Deepen Your Expertise: Advanced Techniques for LLMs

Having grasped the fundamentals of building LLM applications with TensorFlow, it's time to delve into advanced techniques that will elevate your LLM development skills. This section equips you with powerful tools to unlock the full potential of LLMs.

1. Transfer Learning: Leverage Pre-trained Knowledge for Faster Training and Improved Performance
While pre-trained LLMs offer a strong foundation, transfer learning unlocks their true potential for custom applications. Here's how:

Fine-tuning the Powerhouse: This technique involves taking a pre-trained LLM like BART or T5 and adjusting specific layers or hyperparameters. You train the model on your smaller, task-specific dataset, allowing it to leverage its pre-existing knowledge while adapting to your unique requirements. This is particularly beneficial for tasks with limited data, where training a model from scratch might be impractical.

Advantages of Transfer Learning:

Reduced Training Time: By leveraging pre-trained knowledge, transfer learning significantly reduces training time compared to training a model from scratch. This allows for faster experimentation and iteration during development.
Enhanced Performance: Fine-tuning a pre-trained LLM often leads to better performance on your specific task compared to training a new model from scratch,

especially for complex tasks where the LLM can benefit from the general understanding of language it acquired during pre-training.

Example in Action: Imagine you're building a custom LLM for code commenting. You can fine-tune a pre-trained LLM on a massive code dataset, then further refine it on a dataset specifically focused on the programming language and coding domain you're interested in. This allows the LLM to learn the nuances of code structure and commenting practices within that specific domain.

2. Multi-task Learning: Train for Multiple Tasks Simultaneously to Enhance Performance

Multi-task learning allows you to train your LLM on multiple related tasks concurrently. This can be particularly beneficial if the tasks share underlying similarities. Here's the concept at play:

Shared Representations: Power in Similarity: By training on multiple tasks simultaneously, the LLM learns to identify shared representations between the tasks. This improves performance on all tasks compared to training separate models for each individual task. The LLM essentially learns transferable knowledge that can be applied across related domains.

Example: You're building an LLM for a virtual assistant that needs to handle tasks like summarizing news articles, writing emails, and generating different creative text formats. By training the LLM on all these tasks simultaneously through multi-tasking learning, it can learn the nuances of language that are generally applicable across these domains, leading to better performance on each individual task. For instance, the LLM might learn aspects of sentence structure, factual accuracy, and creative phrasing that can be beneficial for all three tasks.

3. Ensemble Learning: Combining Strengths for Superior Performance
Ensemble learning involves combining multiple LLM models with different strengths to create an even more powerful model. Here's the strategy:

Harnessing Diversity is Key: Each LLM model in the ensemble might be trained on different data, with different architectures, or using different hyperparameters. This diversity in training approaches leads to a more robust ensemble model, as it leverages a wider range of perspectives on the task.

Combining Outputs: A Balancing Act: There are various techniques to combine the outputs from the different models within the ensemble. Averaging predictions or using weighted voting are common approaches. Weighted voting assigns higher influence to models that have historically performed better on the specific task.

Benefits of Ensemble Learning:

Improved Accuracy: Ensemble models often outperform individual models by leveraging the unique strengths of each component model. By combining multiple perspectives, the ensemble can arrive at more accurate and reliable outputs.

Reduced Variance: Ensembles can help reduce the variance of the model's predictions, leading to more consistent and reliable outputs. This is because the ensemble is less likely to be overly influenced by specific biases or errors present in any one of the individual models.

Example: You can create an ensemble of LLMs trained with different summarization techniques (e.g., extractive vs. abstractive) to generate more comprehensive and informative summaries. By combining the strengths of different summarization approaches, the ensemble LLM can potentially produce summaries that capture both the key factual content and the overall sentiment of the original text.

These advanced techniques provide powerful tools to enhance your LLM development journey. Remember, the field of LLM development is constantly evolving. Stay updated with the latest advancements in transfer learning, multi-task learning, ensemble methods, and other emerging techniques to push the boundaries of what's possible with LLMs.

6.1. Advanced TensorFlow Techniques for LLM Training

Beyond the foundational steps of building LLM applications with TensorFlow, advanced techniques can significantly enhance the training process, leading to more efficient, performant, and robust models. This section dives into these techniques, empowering you to refine your LLM development skills.

1. Custom Loss Functions: Tailoring Metrics to Your Task
While TensorFlow provides built-in loss functions like cross-entropy for classification tasks, consider creating custom loss functions for specific LLM tasks. Here's why:

Standard Metrics Might Not Capture Nuance: Generic loss functions might not perfectly capture the nuances of your LLM task. For example, in text summarization, you might want to penalize models that deviate from factual accuracy or fail to capture the sentiment of the original text.

Designing a Custom Loss Function:

Identify key aspects you want to optimize in your LLM's outputs. This could be factual accuracy, fluency, creativity, or adherence to a specific style.

Research existing loss functions related to your task and explore how they can be adapted or combined to create a custom metric.

Leverage TensorFlow's flexibility to define custom operations within your loss function using the tf.keras.losses.Loss class.

Example: For a sentiment analysis LLM, you might design a custom loss function that combines a standard cross-entropy term for classification with an additional term penalizing the model for outputs that deviate from the sentiment lexicon used for training.

2. Gradient Clipping: Mitigating Exploding Gradients
Gradient clipping is a technique used to address the vanishing or exploding gradient problem during LLM training. Here's the concept:

Understanding the Problem: In complex models like LLMs, gradients used to update model weights can become very large (explode) or very small (vanish) during backpropagation. This can hinder the training process by causing the model to get stuck in local minima or make erratic updates.

Gradient Clipping in Action: This technique sets a threshold for the gradients. Any gradient exceeding the threshold is clipped to that value, preventing it from exploding and allowing for smoother updates during backpropagation.

Implementation in TensorFlow: TensorFlow provides functionalities like tf.clip_by_value to implement gradient clipping within your training loop.

3. Early Stopping: Preventing Overfitting
Early stopping is a crucial technique to prevent your LLM from overfitting to the training data. Here's how it works:

Overfitting Explained: Overfitting occurs when a model memorizes the training data too well and fails to generalize to unseen data. This can lead to poor performance on real-world tasks.

Early Stopping Strategy: Monitor the model's performance on a validation set during training. If the validation accuracy plateaus or starts to decline, even though training accuracy keeps improving, it's a sign of overfitting. Early stopping halts the training process at this point, preventing the model from memorizing irrelevant details from the training data.

Implementation in TensorFlow: Utilize tools like tf.keras.callbacks.EarlyStopping within your training loop to automatically stop training when the validation performance stops improving for a predefined number of epochs.

4. Mixed Precision Training: Accelerating Training with Reduced Memory Footprint

Mixed precision training leverages a combination of data types during training to accelerate the process and reduce memory usage. Here's the approach:

Balancing Efficiency and Accuracy: Traditionally, LLM training uses float32 data types for calculations, which can be computationally expensive. Mixed precision training allows using a lower precision format like float16 for most computations while maintaining float32 for critical operations, achieving a balance between efficiency and accuracy.

TensorFlow Support: TensorFlow offers built-in support for mixed precision training through the tf.keras.mixed_precision module. This module helps you configure your model and training loop for mixed precision.

Benefits: Mixed precision training can significantly reduce training time and memory usage, especially for large LLMs. This allows for faster experimentation and training on bigger datasets.

5. Gradient Accumulation: Efficient Training with Limited Memory
Gradient accumulation is a technique used when dealing with large LLM models or limited GPU memory. Here's the concept:

Memory Constraints: Training large LLMs can require significant GPU memory to store all the gradients for a single training step. Gradient accumulation addresses this by accumulating gradients over multiple batches before applying them for model updates.

The Accumulation Process: Instead of updating the model weights after each batch, gradients from multiple batches are accumulated. Once enough gradients are accumulated, they are applied in a single update step. This reduces the memory footprint required during training.

Implementation in TensorFlow:

This section dives into the code implementation aspects of various advanced techniques explored previously, providing practical guidance for incorporating them into your TensorFlow LLM training workflows.

1. Custom Loss Functions:

TensorFlow offers flexibility in defining custom loss functions using the tf.keras.losses.Loss class. Here's a basic structure:

Python
```
import tensorflow as tf

class CustomLoss(tf.keras.losses.Loss):

  def __init__(self, alpha, **kwargs):
    super(CustomLoss, self).__init__(**kwargs)
```

```python
        self.alpha = alpha  # Hyperparameter weighting the custom term

    def call(self, y_true, y_pred):
        # Standard loss calculation (e.g., cross-entropy)
        standard_loss = tf.keras.losses.categorical_crossentropy(y_true, y_pred)

        # Custom loss term (replace with your specific logic)
        custom_loss = tf.reduce_mean(tf.abs(y_true - y_pred))  # Example: L1 distance

        # Combine losses with weighting factor (adjust as needed)
        total_loss = standard_loss + self.alpha * custom_loss
        return total_loss
```

Use code with caution.

content_copy

Explanation:

We define a class CustomLoss inheriting from tf.keras.losses.Loss.

The __init__ method initializes any hyperparameters like the weighting factor (alpha) for the custom term.

The call method takes the true labels (y_true) and model predictions (y_pred) as input.

It calculates the standard loss (e.g., cross-entropy) using a built-in TensorFlow loss function.

Define your custom loss term specific to your task (replace the example with your logic).

Combine the standard and custom loss terms with appropriate weighting.
The call method returns the total loss for backpropagation.

2. Gradient Clipping:

TensorFlow provides the tf.clip_by_value function for gradient clipping. Here's how to implement it:

Python
```
optimizer = tf.keras.optimizers.Adam(...)  # Your chosen optimizer

# Clip gradients between -1.0 and 1.0
def clip_gradients(gradients, clip_value):
    clipped_gradients = [tf.clip_by_value(g, -clip_value, clip_value) for g in gradients]
    return clipped_gradients

# Apply clipping during training loop
optimizer.apply_gradients(zip(clip_gradients(model.trainable_variables, 1.0), model.trainable_variables))
```
Use code with caution.
content_copy

Explanation:

We define a function clip_gradients that takes the gradients (gradients) and a clip value (clip_value) as input.

It iterates through the model's trainable variables and applies tf.clip_by_value to each gradient, limiting its value between -clip_value and clip_value.
Within the training loop, after calculating gradients, we use optimizer.apply_gradients with the clipped gradients instead of the original ones.

3. Early Stopping:

TensorFlow provides the tf.keras.callbacks.EarlyStopping callback for early stopping. Here's an example:

Python
```python
early_stopping = tf.keras.callbacks.EarlyStopping(
    monitor='val_accuracy',  # Metric to monitor (adjust as needed)
    patience=5,   # Number of epochs to wait for improvement
    restore_best_weights=True   # Restore best model weights
)

model.fit(..., callbacks=[early_stopping])
```
Use code with caution.
content_copy

Explanation:

We create an EarlyStopping callback instance.

We specify the metric to monitor (val_accuracy in this case) and the number of epochs (patience) to wait for improvement on the validation set before stopping.
Setting restore_best_weights=True ensures the model with the best validation performance is loaded at the end of training.
We pass the early_stopping callback within the callbacks list to the model.fit function.

4. Mixed Precision Training:

TensorFlow offers the tf.keras.mixed_precision module for mixed precision training. Here's a simplified setup:

```python
Python
from tensorflow.keras.mixed_precision import Policy

policy = Policy('mixed_float16')    # Choose an appropriate policy
precision_loss = policy.compute_loss(loss_fn)  # Wrap loss function

model.compile(optimizer=..., loss=precision_loss)
Use code with caution.
content_copy
```

Explanation:

We import the Policy class from tf.keras.mixed_precision.

We create a Policy instance, specifying the mixed precision policy to use. Different policies might be available depending on your hardware capabilities. Consult the TensorFlowdocumentation for recommended policies.

We use the compute_loss method of the policy to wrap our existing loss function (loss_fn). This ensures the loss calculation leverages the chosen mixed precision policy.
During model compilation, we specify the wrapped precision_loss function instead of the original loss function.
Finally, we train our model using the compiled model with mixed precision enabled

6.2. Optimizing Performance and Efficiency of LLM Models

Large Language Models (LLMs) hold immense potential for revolutionizing various fields. However, their training and deployment can be computationally expensive and resource-intensive. To unlock the full potential of LLMs, optimizing their performance and efficiency is crucial. This guide explores various techniques to achieve this goal.

1. Strategic Model Architecture Selection:

Choosing the Right Architecture: The LLM architecture plays a significant role in performance and efficiency. Consider factors like task requirements, available resources, and desired trade-off between accuracy and speed. Transformer-based architectures like T5 or BART are powerful but require significant resources. Alternatives like efficient transformers or compressed transformers can offer a good balance for specific tasks.

2. Data Optimization Techniques:

Data Quality and Relevance: Ensure your training data is high-quality, relevant to your LLM's task, and free from biases. This directly impacts the model's performance and efficiency. Techniques like data cleaning, filtering, and augmentation can improve data quality.

Data Augmentation: Artificially expand your dataset using techniques like synonym replacement, back-translation (for multilingual tasks), or paraphrasing. This helps the LLM generalize better and potentially reduces training time.

3. Training Optimization Techniques:

Leveraging Pre-trained Models: Pre-trained LLMs like those available on TensorFlow Hub can serve as a robust starting point. Fine-tuning these models on your specific task and data can significantly reduce training time and improve performance compared to training from scratch.

Transfer Learning: Utilize transfer learning techniques to transfer knowledge gained by a pre-trained LLM on a similar task to your specific task. This can lead to faster training and improved performance on your target domain.

Gradient Clipping and Early Stopping: Gradient clipping mitigates exploding gradients during training, leading to smoother optimization and potentially faster convergence. Early stopping prevents overfitting by halting training when the model's performance on a validation set plateaus.

Mixed Precision Training: As discussed earlier, mixed precision training leverages a mix of data types (e.g., float16 and float32) during training. This can significantly accelerate training times and reduce memory usage, especially for large LLMs.

4. Hardware and Software Optimization:

Hardware Acceleration: Utilize hardware with dedicated support for deep learning computations, such as GPUs or TPUs (Tensor Processing Units). These accelerators can significantly improve training and inference speeds. Model Pruning and Quantization: Techniques like model pruning and quantization can reduce the model size and computational complexity. Pruning removes redundant connections, while quantization reduces the precision of weights and activations, leading to smaller model footprints and potentially faster inference. However, these techniques might require careful tuning to avoid sacrificing accuracy.

5. Efficient Inference Techniques:

Efficient Model Selection: When deploying your LLM, consider using a more efficient model architecture specifically designed for inference. These models might trade some accuracy for faster runtime performance. Batching and Tiling: Process multiple inputs simultaneously (batching) or divide the input into smaller chunks (tiling) for efficient utilization of hardware resources during inference.

Knowledge Distillation: Train a smaller, faster model to mimic the behavior of a larger, more accurate model. This allows for faster and more efficient inference while preserving the knowledge of the original model.

Remember: Optimizing LLM performance and efficiency is an iterative process. Experiment with different techniques, monitor results closely, and fine-tune your approach to achieve the best balance between performance, efficiency, and resource constraints for your specific LLM application.

6.3. Debugging and Troubleshooting Common LLM Issues

Large Language Models (LLMs) are powerful tools, but like any complex system, they can encounter issues during development and deployment. This guide equips you with strategies to debug and troubleshoot common LLM problems, ensuring your models function optimally.

1. Performance Issues:

Low Accuracy or Poor Outputs:

Analyze Training Data: Ensure your training data is high-quality, relevant to the task, and free from biases. Consider data cleaning, augmentation, or incorporating additional relevant data sources.

Model Architecture Selection: Re-evaluate your chosen LLM architecture. For specific tasks, efficient transformers or compressed transformers might offer a better balance between accuracy and resource usage compared to larger models.

Training Hyperparameter Tuning: Experiment with hyperparameters like learning rate, optimizer settings, or batch size. Inappropriate hyperparameters can hinder learning and lead to subpar performance.
Slow Training Times:

Utilize Pre-trained Models: Leverage pre-trained models and fine-tune them for your specific task. This can significantly reduce training time compared to training from scratch.

Mixed Precision Training: Implement mixed precision training to accelerate training by using a mix of data types (e.g., float16 and float32) during computations.
Hardware Optimization: Ensure you're using hardware with dedicated deep learning support like GPUs or TPUs. These accelerators can significantly improve training speeds.

2. Training Issues:

Model Overfitting:

Early Stopping: Implement early stopping to halt training when the model's performance on a validation set plateaus. This prevents the model from memorizing irrelevant details from the training data.

Data Augmentation: Artificially expand your training data using techniques like synonym replacement, back-translation, or paraphrasing. This helps the model generalize better and potentially reduces overfitting.
L1/L2 Regularization: Apply L1 or L2 regularization techniques during training. These penalize large weights, promoting simpler models that are less prone to overfitting.

Training Not Converging:

Gradient Clipping: Implement gradient clipping to mitigate exploding gradients during training. This can lead to smoother optimization and potentially help the model converge.

Learning Rate Tuning: Adjust the learning rate. An excessively high learning rate can cause the model to oscillate and never converge, while a very low rate can lead to slow learning.

3. Inference Issues:

Inaccurate or Irrelevant Outputs During Inference:
Evaluate Model Generalizability: Ensure your model generalizes well to unseen data beyond the training set. Consider incorporating diverse data sources during training.

Knowledge Distillation: Train a smaller model to mimic the behavior of a larger, more accurate model. This can improve inference performance while preserving the knowledge of the original model.

4. Debugging Techniques:

Logging and Monitoring: Implement comprehensive logging and monitoring practices during training and inference. Track metrics like loss, accuracy, and resource utilization to identify potential issues early on. Tools like TensorBoard can be invaluable for visualization and analysis.

Gradient Checking: Verify that gradients are flowing correctly through your model. Erratic or vanishing gradients can hinder training.
Model Visualization Techniques: Techniques like attention visualization can provide insights into the model's internal workings and help identify potential biases or decision-making patterns.

Remember: Debugging LLMs is an ongoing process. By systematically analyzing performance issues, employing appropriate techniques, and leveraging debugging tools, you can effectively troubleshoot problems and ensure your LLMs function optimally. As the field of LLMs evolves, stay updated on the latest debugging and troubleshooting best practices to maintain the effectiveness of your models.

VII. Beyond TensorFlow: Integrating Hugging Face and Other Tools

While TensorFlow provides a robust foundation for building and training LLMs, the LLM development landscape offers a rich ecosystem of complementary tools and libraries. This section explores how you can integrate Hugging Face and other valuable tools to enhance your LLM development process.

1. Hugging Face Transformers: Pre-trained Models and Ecosystem

Hugging Face Transformers is a prominent library offering a vast collection of pre-trained LLM models, evaluation metrics, and fine-tuning utilities. Here's how it empowers your LLM development:

Pre-trained LLM Zoo: Access a diverse collection of pre-trained LLM models like BART, T5, or XLNet, all readily available for fine-tuning on your specific tasks. This significantly reduces training time and effort compared to training from scratch.

Fine-tuning Made Easy: Hugging Face Transformers provides functionalities for seamlessly fine-tuning pre-trained models on your custom datasets. This allows you to leverage the pre-trained knowledge while adapting the model to your specific domain and task.

Evaluation Metrics: Explore various task-specific evaluation metrics available through Hugging Face Transformers. These metrics go beyond basic accuracy and provide insights into the quality and relevance of your model's outputs.

2. Integration with TensorFlow:

Hugging Face Transformers models can be seamlessly integrated into your TensorFlow LLM development workflows. Here's how:

TensorFlow Compatibility: Hugging Face Transformers models are designed to be compatible with TensorFlow. You can load pre-trained models and fine-tune them within your TensorFlow training scripts.

Keras Integration: Hugging Face Transformers models can be used as layers within your Keras models built in TensorFlow. This allows for flexible integration and customization.

3. Additional Tools for Enhanced LLM Development:

Beyond TensorFlow and Hugging Face Transformers, explore these valuable tools to streamline your LLM development journey:

Datasets and Data Preprocessing: Utilize libraries like Apache Arrow or datasets from Hugging Face Hub for efficient data access and manipulation. Tools like TensorFlow Text can simplify text preprocessing tasks.

Visualization Tools: Tools like TensorBoard (integrated with TensorFlow) or libraries like MLflow can be invaluable for visualizing training progress, monitoring metrics, and debugging issues.

Cloud Platforms: Consider cloud platforms like Google Cloud AI Platform or Amazon SageMaker that offer pre-built infrastructure for training, deploying, and managing LLMs. These platforms can simplify deployment and scaling processes.

4. Continuous Learning and Improvement:

Stay Updated: The LLM landscape is constantly evolving. Regularly explore new pre-trained models, evaluation metrics, and techniques from Hugging Face and the broader machine learning community.

Experimentation is Key: Don't be afraid to experiment with different architectures, pre-trained models, hyperparameter combinations, and tools. This continuous exploration leads to the discovery of optimal solutions for your specific LLM application.

By embracing TensorFlow, Hugging Face Transformers, and other relevant tools, you can unlock the full potential of LLM development. Remember, the most effective approach often involves a combination of these tools, tailored to your specific LLM project requirements. So, keep exploring, keep experimenting, and keep pushing the boundaries of what's possible with LLMs!

7.1. Utilizing Hugging Face Transformers for LLM Development

Large Language Models (LLMs) have revolutionized various fields, and Hugging Face Transformers has emerged as a powerful toolkit for LLM development. This guide delves into how you can leverage Hugging Face Transformers to streamline your LLM development process, boost efficiency, and achieve impressive results.

1. The Power of Pre-trained Models: A Head Start for Your LLM

Hugging Face Transformers offers a treasure trove of pre-trained LLM models, serving as a launchpad for your LLM development journey. These models, like BART, T5, or XLNet, have been trained on massive amounts of text data, allowing them to capture complex linguistic relationships and perform various tasks like text summarization, question answering, or code generation.

Benefits of Pre-trained Models:

Reduced Training Time: By leveraging pre-trained models, you significantly reduce the training time required compared to training a model from scratch. This allows for faster experimentation and quicker deployment of your LLM application.

Improved Performance: Pre-trained models encode valuable knowledge from vast datasets, often leading to superior performance on specific tasks compared to models trained on smaller datasets.

Focus on Fine-tuning: With the pre-trained foundation laid, you can focus your efforts on fine-tuning the model for your specific task and data. This involves adjusting specific layers or hyperparameters to optimize the model's performance for your unique needs.

2. Seamless Fine-tuning: Tailoring the LLM to Your Task

Hugging Face Transformers simplifies the fine-tuning process, allowing you to efficiently adapt pre-trained models to your specific task and data. Here's how:

Intuitive API: Hugging Face Transformers provides a user-friendly API for loading pre-trained models and fine-tuning them on your custom datasets. This eliminates the need for complex code from scratch.

Transfer Learning in Action: Fine-tuning leverages the pre-trained knowledge of the model as a starting point. You then fine-tune specific layers or parameters to specialize the model for your task, essentially transferring learned knowledge to your domain.

K3. Evaluation Metrics: Measuring Success Beyond Accuracy

Hugging Face Transformers goes beyond basic accuracy metrics and offers various task-specific evaluation metrics to assess the quality and relevance of your LLM's outputs. Here are some examples:

Text Summarization: Metrics like ROUGE score evaluate how well your model captures the main points and factual content of the original text in the generated summary.
Question Answering: Metrics like BLEU score assess how closely the generated answer matches a human-written reference answer.

Machine Translation: BLEU score can also be used here to measure the fluency and fidelity of the translated text compared to a human translation.
4. Integration with TensorFlow for a Powerful Workflow

Hugging Face Transformers models seamlessly integrate with TensorFlow, allowing you to leverage the strengths of both frameworks:

TensorFlow Compatibility: Hugging Face Transformers models can be loaded and fine-tuned directly within your TensorFlow training scripts. This enables you to leverage TensorFlow's capabilities for building and training complex models.

Keras Integration: Hugging Face Transformers models can be used as building blocks within your Keras models built in TensorFlow. This allows for flexible integration and customization of your LLM architecture.

5. A Look Beyond: Complementary Tools for Enhanced Development

While Hugging Face Transformers offers a powerful foundation, consider incorporating these additional tools to further optimize your LLM development:

Datasets and Preprocessing: Explore tools like Apache Arrow or datasets from Hugging Face Hub for efficient data access and manipulation. Additionally, TensorFlow Text can simplify text preprocessing tasks like tokenization and cleaning.

Visualization Tools: Tools like TensorBoard (integrated with TensorFlow) or libraries like MLflow can be invaluable for visualizing training progress, monitoring metrics like loss and accuracy, and identifying potential issues during training.

Cloud Platforms: Consider cloud platforms like Google Cloud AI Platform or Amazon SageMaker that offer pre-built infrastructure for training, deploying, and managing LLMs. These platforms can simplify deployment processes and provide scalability for large-scale models.

Embrace the Potential: Experimentation is Key

The LLM development landscape is constantly evolving. Don't be afraid to experiment with different pre-trained models, evaluation metrics, hyperparameter combinations, and tools offered by Hugging Face Transformers and the broader machine learning community. This continuous exploration will lead you to discover the optimal solutions for your specific LLM application and unlock the full potential of LLMs.

By leveraging the power of Hugging Face Transformers and its rich ecosystem of tools, you can streamline your LLM development process, achieve superior results, and contribute to the cutting edge of LLM technology.

7.2. Exploring Additional Libraries and Frameworks for LLMs

While TensorFlow and Hugging Face Transformers form a formidable duo for LLM development, the landscape offers a wealth of additional libraries and frameworks catering to various aspects of the LLM development process. Here's a glimpse into some valuable tools you can explore alongside these core technologies:

1. Jax and Flax for High-Performance Experimentation:

Focus on Numerical Computation: Jax, a high-performance numerical computation library from Google Research, excels at automatic differentiation and just-in-time (JIT) compilation. This translates to efficient experimentation and rapid prototyping for LLM development.

Flax, the Jax-based Deep Learning Library: Flax builds upon Jax, specifically designed for building and training neural networks. It provides a concise and functional API for constructing and manipulating LLM architectures, making it suitable for rapid experimentation.

2. PyTorch for Flexibility and Customization:

Dynamic Computation Graph: PyTorch, a popular deep learning framework, offers a dynamic computation graph. This allows for greater flexibility in defining and manipulating the model architecture during training, which can be beneficial for certain LLM research projects.

Large Community and Extensive Ecosystem: PyTorch boasts a vast and active community, along with a rich ecosystem of libraries and tools. This can be helpful for finding solutions and support for specific challenges you might encounter during LLM development.

3. SpaCy for Advanced Natural Language Processing (NLP) Tasks:

Industrial-Strength NLP Toolkit: SpaCy is a powerful industrial-strength NLP library that offers a comprehensive suite of tools for tasks like tokenization, named entity recognition (NER), and dependency parsing. These functionalities can be valuable for preprocessing text data and enriching your LLM models with deeper linguistic understanding.

4. FastAPI for Building User-Friendly LLM APIs:

Rapid API Development: FastAPI is a high-performance web framework that excels in building APIs. This can be instrumental in deploying your LLM as a web service, allowing users to interact with your LLM through a user-friendly interface.

Focus on Developer Experience: FastAPI prioritizes developer experience, offering a clean and concise syntax for building APIs. This simplifies the process of deploying your LLM and making it accessible to others.

5. Streamlit for Interactive LLM Applications:

Create Interactive Demos: Streamlit is another web framework that allows you to quickly build interactive web applications. This can be useful for creating demos or exploratory interfaces for your LLM, enabling users to experiment with its capabilities in a real-time setting.

Choosing the Right Tools for Your Needs:

The optimal choice of libraries and frameworks depends on your specific LLM project requirements and preferences. Here's a breakdown to guide your selection:

TensorFlow + Hugging Face Transformers: Ideal for a robust foundation, pre-trained models, and TensorFlow integration.

Jax + Flax: Excellent for high-performance experimentation and rapid prototyping.
PyTorch: Well-suited for projects requiring flexibility in model architecture and leveraging a large community.

SpaCy: Invaluable for advanced NLP tasks and enriching your LLM with deeper linguistic understanding.
FastAPI: Perfect for building user-friendly APIs to deploy your LLM as a web service.

Streamlit: Great for creating interactive demos or exploratory interfaces for your LLM.

Remember: Don't hesitate to explore and experiment with different tools throughout your LLM development journey. By leveraging the strengths of various libraries and frameworks, you can build powerful, efficient, and user-friendly LLM applications that push the boundaries of what's possible.

7.2. Exploring Additional Libraries and Frameworks for LLMs

Expanding Your LLM Development Toolkit: Powerful Libraries and Frameworks Beyond TensorFlow and Hugging Face

While TensorFlow and Hugging Face Transformers provide a robust foundation for LLM development, the landscape offers a treasure trove of additional libraries and frameworks catering to specific aspects of the LLM development process. Here, we delve into some of these valuable tools that can empower you to create even more powerful and effective LLM applications.

1. Jax and Flax for High-Performance Experimentation:

Focus on Speed and Efficiency: Jax, a high-performance numerical computation library developed by Google Research, excels in automatic differentiation and just-in-time (JIT) compilation. This translates to significant speed advantages, making Jax ideal for rapid prototyping and experimentation during LLM development.

Flax: Streamlined Deep Learning on Jax: Flax builds upon Jax, specifically designed for building and training neural networks. It provides a concise and functional API for constructing and manipulating LLM architectures, making it particularly suitable for rapid exploration of different LLM configurations.

2. PyTorch for Flexibility and Customization:

Dynamic Computation Graphs: PyTorch, another popular deep learning framework, offers a dynamic computation graph. This allows for greater flexibility in defining and manipulating the model architecture during training. This dynamic nature can be beneficial for certain LLM research projects where the model architecture might evolve iteratively.

Large Community and Extensive Ecosystem: PyTorch boasts a vast and active community, along with a rich ecosystem of libraries and tools. This can be extremely helpful when encountering challenges during LLM development, as you'll have access to a wealth of resources and support from other developers.

3. SpaCy for Advanced Natural Language Processing (NLP) Tasks:

Industrial-Strength NLP Toolkit: SpaCy is a powerful industrial-strength NLP library that offers a comprehensive suite of tools for tasks like tokenization, named entity recognition (NER), and dependency parsing. These functionalities can be valuable for preprocessing text data and enriching your LLM models with a deeper understanding of language structure and relationships. This deeper linguistic understanding can lead to more nuanced and accurate outputs from your LLM.

4. FastAPI for User-Friendly LLM APIs:

Rapid API Development: FastAPI is a high-performance web framework that excels in building APIs. This can be instrumental in deploying your LLM as a web service, allowing users to interact with your LLM through a user-friendly interface. FastAPI streamlines the process of creating APIs, enabling you to share your LLM's capabilities with a wider audience.

Focus on Developer Experience: FastAPI prioritizes developer experience, offering a clean and concise syntax for building APIs. This simplifies the process of deploying your LLM and making it accessible to others.

5. Streamlit for Interactive LLM Applications:

Create Interactive Demos: Streamlit is another web framework that allows you to quickly build interactive web applications. This can be useful for creating demos or exploratory interfaces for your LLM, enabling users to experiment with its capabilities in a real-time setting. Streamlit applications can be a great way to showcase the functionality of your LLM and gather user feedback.

Choosing the Right Tools for Your Project:

The optimal choice of libraries and frameworks depends on your specific LLM project requirements and preferences. Here's a breakdown to guide your selection:

TensorFlow + Hugging Face Transformers: Ideal for a robust foundation, pre-trained models, and TensorFlow integration.

Jax + Flax: Excellent for high-performance experimentation and rapid prototyping.

PyTorch: Well-suited for projects requiring flexibility in model architecture and leveraging a large community.

SpaCy: Invaluable for advanced NLP tasks and enriching your LLM with deeper linguistic understanding.

FastAPI: Perfect for building user-friendly APIs to deploy your LLM as a web service.

Streamlit: Great for creating interactive demos or exploratory interfaces for your LLM.

Remember: Don't be afraid to explore and experiment with different tools throughout your LLM development journey. By leveraging the strengths of various libraries and frameworks, you can build powerful, efficient, and user-friendly LLM applications that push the boundaries of what's possible in the field of large language models. Stay curious, keep learning, and continue to explore the ever-evolving landscape of LLM development tools!

VIII. The Future of LLMs and TensorFlow

Large Language Models (LLMs) and TensorFlow are poised to shape the future of artificial intelligence, with exciting advancements anticipated on the horizon. Here, we explore the potential directions of this collaborative journey:

1. Enhanced LLM Capabilities:

Lifelong Learning: Future LLMs might possess the ability to continuously learn and update their knowledge base, similar to how humans learn throughout their lives. This could involve techniques like continual learning or reinforcement learning, allowing LLMs to adapt to new information and improve their performance over time.

Reasoning and Commonsense Knowledge Integration: LLMs might evolve to incorporate reasoning abilities and commonsense knowledge, enabling them to go beyond simple text generation or pattern recognition. This would allow them to understand the context of a situation, draw logical conclusions, and provide more comprehensive responses.

Explainability and Transparency: Increased interpretability and explainability of LLM decision-making are crucial for trust and adoption. Future advancements might involve techniques like attention visualization or model introspection, allowing users to understand the rationale behind the LLM's outputs.

2. TensorFlow's Role in LLM Evolution:

Efficient Training and Scalability: TensorFlow is expected to play a key role in enabling the training of even larger and more complex LLMs. Advancements in distributed training, mixed precision training, and hardware optimization will be crucial for handling the computational demands of these next-generation models.

Focus on User-Friendliness: TensorFlow is likely to become even more user-friendly, offering simplified APIs and tools specifically designed for LLM development. This will lower the barrier to entry for developers and researchers, accelerating the pace of LLM innovation.

Integration with Other Tools: Seamless integration with other frameworks like Jax or PyTorch, as well as NLP libraries like SpaCy, could become more commonplace within TensorFlow. This would allow developers to leverage the strengths of various tools within a unified workflow.

3. Real-World Applications:

Personalized Education: LLMs could personalize learning experiences, tailoring educational content and guidance to individual student needs and learning styles.
Scientific Discovery: LLMs could assist researchers in scientific fields by analyzing vast amounts of data, identifying patterns, and formulating new hypotheses.
Human-Machine Collaboration: LLMs could become powerful tools for human-machine collaboration, assisting in tasks like writing, translation, or code generation.

Challenges and Considerations:

Bias and Fairness: As LLMs become more powerful, addressing potential biases and ensuring fair treatment across different demographics will be critical. Techniques for mitigating bias in training data and model design will be crucial.

Safety and Security: Safeguarding against potential misuse of LLMs, such as the spread of misinformation or the creation of harmful content, will require careful consideration. Robust safety measures and responsible development practices will be essential.
Explainability and Transparency: As mentioned earlier, ensuring users understand how LLMs arrive at their outputs will be crucial for trust and responsible deployment.

The Future is Collaborative:

The future of LLMs and TensorFlow is a collaborative journey. By leveraging the strengths of both, researchers and developers can create powerful and versatile LLMs that address real-world challenges and empower humans in various domains. As we move forward, addressing ethical considerations and ensuring responsible development will be paramount in shaping a future where LLMs contribute positively to society.

8.1. Emerging Trends and Advancements in LLM Technology

Large Language Models (LLMs) are rapidly evolving, pushing the boundaries of what's possible in artificial intelligence. Here, we delve into some of the most exciting emerging trends and advancements shaping the future of LLM technology:

1. Lifelong Learning LLMs:

Moving Beyond Static Models: Traditional LLMs are trained on massive datasets but lack the ability to continuously learn and update their knowledge. The future lies in LLMs that can incorporate new information and adapt over time, similar to how humans learn.

Continual Learning and Reinforcement Learning: Techniques like continual learning allow LLMs to learn from new data streams without forgetting previously acquired knowledge. Reinforcement learning approaches can further enhance this process by enabling LLMs to learn through trial and error interactions with their environment.

2. Enhanced Reasoning and Commonsense Integration:

Beyond Pattern Recognition: Current LLMs excel at pattern recognition but often struggle with tasks requiring reasoning or commonsense knowledge. Future advancements aim to equip LLMs with the ability to understand context, draw logical conclusions, and make inferences based on real-world knowledge.

Symbolic AI and Knowledge Graphs: Integrating symbolic AI techniques and knowledge graphs encoded with factual information could empower LLMs to reason and solve problems more effectively. This would allow them to go beyond simple text generation and perform more complex tasks.

3. Increased Explainability and Transparency:

Building Trust Through Transparency: As LLMs become more powerful, ensuring users understand how they arrive at their outputs is crucial for trust and responsible deployment. Techniques like attention visualization or model introspection could shed light on the rationale behind an LLM's decision-making process.

Interpretable Machine Learning Methods: Research in interpretable machine learning is crucial for developing LLMs that can explain their reasoning and provide insights into their thought processes. This will be essential for fostering user trust and addressing potential biases in LLM outputs.

4. Multimodal Learning and Embodied Cognition:

Beyond Text Data: LLMs are traditionally trained on text data. Future advancements aim to incorporate other modalities like images, audio, or video. This would enable LLMs to understand and generate information across different formats, leading to a more holistic understanding of the world.

Embodied Cognition for Situated Understanding: Integrating embodied cognition principles could allow LLMs to learn from interactions with the physical world. This would enable them to perform tasks that require understanding the real-world context, such as robot navigation or manipulation.

5. Hardware and Software Co-design:

Optimizing for LLM Development: Hardware advancements like specialized AI accelerators and neuromorphic computing architectures are crucial for efficiently training and running ever-larger LLMs. Software advancements in areas like distributed training and model compression will also play a vital role.

Co-designing for Efficiency and Scalability: A collaborative effort between hardware and software developers will be essential to optimize the entire LLM development process. This co-design approach will ensure efficient training, faster inference times, and the ability to handle increasingly complex LLM architectures.

The Road Ahead

These emerging trends represent a glimpse into the exciting future of LLM technology. As researchers and developers continue to push boundaries, LLMs have the potential to revolutionize various fields, from scientific discovery and personalized education to human-machine collaboration and creative content generation. However, addressing ethical considerations like bias, safety, and transparency will be paramount in ensuring responsible development and deployment of these powerful AI systems. By embracing these advancements and fostering a collaborative approach, we can shape a future where LLMs empower humans and contribute positively to society.

8.2. The Impact of LLMs on Various Industries and Applications

Large Language Models (LLMs) are rapidly transforming numerous industries, injecting a wave of automation, creativity, and efficiency across various applications. Let's explore the profound impact LLMs are having and their potential to reshape the future:

1. Redefining Content Creation:

Enhanced Marketing and Advertising: LLMs can personalize marketing materials, generate targeted ad copy, and analyze customer sentiment to optimize marketing campaigns. They can also create engaging product descriptions and social media content, streamlining content creation workflows.

Journalism and Media: LLMs can assist journalists by summarizing news articles, fact-checking information, and even generating initial drafts of reports. They can personalize news feeds and curate content tailored to user interests.

2. Revolutionizing Customer Service:

Intelligent Chatbots and Virtual Assistants: LLMs are powering the development of more sophisticated chatbots that can engage in natural conversations, answer customer queries effectively, and even troubleshoot basic issues. This can significantly improve customer service response times and provide 24/7 support.

Sentiment Analysis and Personalized Support: LLMs can analyze customer interactions, identify emotions and sentiment, and personalize customer support experiences. This allows businesses to address customer concerns more effectively and proactively.

3. Empowering Scientific Research and Development:

Drug Discovery and Material Science: LLMs can analyze vast amounts of scientific data, identify patterns, and generate hypotheses to accelerate scientific discovery. They can aid in material science research by suggesting new material combinations with desired properties.

Personalized Medicine and Healthcare: LLMs can analyze patient data and medical literature to assist doctors in diagnosis and treatment planning. They can personalize treatment plans based on individual patient characteristics and medical history.

4. Transforming Education and Training:

Personalized Learning Experiences: LLMs can personalize learning materials and adapt to individual student needs and learning styles. They can provide real-time feedback and answer student questions in a comprehensive manner, creating a more engaging learning experience.

Intelligent Tutoring Systems: LLMs can power intelligent tutoring systems that can identify student weaknesses, provide targeted support, and adjust the difficulty level of learning materials based on student progress.

5. Shaping the Future of Creative Industries:

Content Generation and Design: LLMs can generate different creative text formats, from poems and scripts to musical pieces. They can also be used for graphic design tasks, assisting in creating layouts and generating image variations based on user input.
Human-Machine Collaboration: LLMs can collaborate with human creators, assisting with tasks like writing, editing, and brainstorming new ideas. This can streamline creative workflows and unlock new creative possibilities.

A Look Ahead: The Potential for Broader Impact

The impact of LLMs extends far beyond these examples. As LLM technology matures, we can expect even more transformative applications in areas like legal research, software development, and financial analysis. However, it's crucial to acknowledge the potential challenges:

Bias and Fairness: LLMs trained on biased data can perpetuate those biases. Addressing bias in training data and model design is essential to ensure fair and ethical use of LLMs.

Job displacement: Automation powered by LLMs might lead to job displacement in certain sectors. It's crucial to focus on reskilling and upskilling initiatives to prepare the workforce for the changing landscape.

In conclusion, LLMs are a powerful force shaping the future of various industries and applications. By embracing their potential while addressing the challenges, we can harness LLMs to create a more efficient, creative, and knowledge-driven world.

8.3. Ethical Considerations and Responsible Development of LLMs

Large Language Models (LLMs) hold immense potential to revolutionize various fields. However, their power necessitates careful consideration of ethical implications to ensure responsible development and deployment. Here, we delve into some key ethical considerations and best practices for building LLMs that benefit society:

1. Bias and Fairness:

Mitigating Bias in Training Data: LLMs trained on biased data can perpetuate those biases in their outputs. It's crucial to employ techniques like data cleaning, augmentation, and incorporating diverse datasets to mitigate bias and promote fair treatment across different demographics.

Algorithmic Bias Detection: Implementing fairness metrics and bias detection algorithms during LLM development can help identify and address potential biases within the model itself.

2. Transparency and Explainability:

Understanding Model Reasoning: As LLMs become more complex, understanding their decision-making processes becomes crucial. Techniques like attention visualization or model introspection can shed light on how LLMs arrive at their outputs, fostering trust and transparency.

Explainable AI Methods: Research in explainable AI (XAI) is essential for developing LLMs that can explain their reasoning and provide insights into their thought processes. This transparency allows users to understand the rationale behind the LLM's outputs and builds trust.

3. Safety and Security:

Mitigating Misinformation and Malicious Use: LLMs can be misused to generate deepfakes, spread misinformation, or create harmful content. Implementing safeguards like fact-checking mechanisms and robust safety filters can help mitigate these risks.
Human Oversight and Control: LLMs should not operate in a black box. Maintaining human oversight and control mechanisms ensures responsible use of LLMs and allows for intervention when necessary.

4. Privacy and Security:

Data Protection and Anonymization: If LLMs are trained on personally identifiable information (PII) data, robust privacy-preserving techniques like anonymization or differential privacy are essential to protect user privacy.

Data Security Measures: Implementing robust data security measures safeguards training data from unauthorized access or manipulation, preventing potential security breaches.

5. Environmental Impact:

Energy Efficiency in Training: Training LLMs often requires significant computing power, leading to high energy consumption. Research into energy-efficient training algorithms and hardware optimization techniques can help minimize the environmental impact of LLM development.

The Road to Responsible Development

Developing and deploying LLMs ethically requires a collaborative effort from researchers, developers, policymakers, and the public. Here are some best practices to promote responsible development:

Open Dialogue and Collaboration: Fostering open dialogue and collaboration between stakeholders is essential to identify and address ethical considerations throughout the LLM development lifecycle.

Public Education and Awareness: Raising public awareness about the capabilities and limitations of

LLMs can foster trust and responsible use of this technology.
Developing Ethical Guidelines: Establishing clear ethical guidelines and best practices for LLM development can provide a framework for researchers and developers to follow.

Conclusion

By prioritizing ethical considerations and embracing responsible development practices, we can ensure that LLMs become a force for good in society. By mitigating bias, promoting transparency, and safeguarding against potential misuse, we can unlock the immense potential of LLMs while ensuring they contribute to a more just, equitable, and sustainable future. Let's harness the power of LLMs responsibly and work together to shape a future where humans and AI collaborate for the benefit of all.

www.ingramcontent.com/pod-product-compliance
Lightning Source LLC
LaVergne TN
LVHW051655050326
832903LV00032B/3836